THE
MOUNT STEWART MURDER

THE
MOUNT
STEWART
MURDER

A RE-EXAMINATION OF THE UK'S OLDEST UNSOLVED MURDER CASE

CHRIS PATON

The
History
Press

To my wife Claire,
and sons Calum and Jamie.

First published 2012

The History Press
The Mill, Brimscombe Port
Stroud, Gloucestershire, GL5 2QG
www.thehistorypress.co.uk

© Chris Paton, 2012

The right of Chris Paton to be identified as the Author
of this work has been asserted in accordance with the
Copyrights, Designs and Patents Act 1988.

British Library Cataloguing in Publication Data.
A catalogue record for this book is available from the British Library.

ISBN 978 0 7524 6020 8

Typesetting and origination by The History Press
Printed in Great Britain

Contents

INTRODUCTION

In 1866, a brutal murder was carried out on the outskirts of the quiet Perthshire village of Forgandenny. While the story may not be familiar to many today, at the time it was widely reported as one of the most horrific killings of the Victorian era. The nature of the murder, the fear within the local community, and the difficulties encountered by the investigative team attempting to solve the crime were all followed meticulously by newspaper readers across the British Isles.

I first became aware of the tragic events at Mount Stewart Farm in early 2002, following a decision to research my family history. Working my way back through birth, marriage and death records at the Edinburgh-based General Register Office for Scotland, it was not long before I discovered that my three times great-grandmother Janet Rogers (*née* Henderson) had passed away on Friday, 30 March 1866. For some time I had no clue as to the actual cause of her death; the area on the certificate which should have stated this was curiously blank. At the time I was a fairly green amateur family historian and had not realised the significance of three letters, 'RCE', written on the left side of the document. If I had done so, I would have immediately realised that I would need to consult the 'Register of Corrected Entries', a volume where additions and corrections to such records could later be made. This would have revealed that Janet's death had been caused as a result of 'injuries inflicted on the head by someone unknown'.

What I lacked in experience as a family historian at this stage I fortunately made up for in enthusiasm. Almost from the start I had posted my genealogical discoveries onto a dedicated website in the hope of luring prospective cousins to help add flesh to the bones. As a strategy it worked for many lines of my research, but it was not to be a relative who would eventually set me on the right course with Janet's story. A teacher called Greg Ross from Strathallan School in Forgandenny emailed me in March 2002 to say that he had discovered my website whilst researching a history of the local parish. He explained that he could provide me with some additional information about my ancestor, for whilst browsing through several Perthshire newspapers he had uncovered the cause of her death – Janet Rogers had been brutally murdered.

Before sending me a copy of the newspaper coverage, Greg forewarned that I might find the report shocking. Janet was a direct ancestor of mine, and on that level it was of course a disturbing read; and yet, upon reading the story, my first impression was perhaps surprisingly not one of shock at all. At the time I was working as a documentary maker at the BBC in Glasgow, primarily on historically based television programmes. As someone who was constantly having to compromise on how much of a story could be told within short television accounts, my initial reaction was one of sheer incredulity at the reportage. Not a detail was omitted about the discovery of her body, and in my mind's eye I could easily picture my poor ancestor's body being found at the scene of the crime. Far from being disturbed, I was instead utterly fascinated, and at the earliest opportunity I drove to Perth to try to find more localised coverage. At the A.K. Bell Library, I successfully located additional newspaper reports of the event, which traced the investigation over the course of the next year. I now found myself with the physicians during the post-mortem examination; I saw the expressions on the faces of witnesses with every question asked; and I felt the very fear of the community in response to the ordeal. Through these articles I was transported back to the realities of life in everyday Victorian Scotland, and I wanted to explore that world further.

Since then I have continued to gather documentary material about the case from additional newspaper coverage, contemporary letters, court papers and more from archives across Scotland, notably in Perth, Dundee and Edinburgh. Initially, the tale that held my interest was the tragedy of the killing itself, but, as time progressed, other stories would soon emerge. The Scotland of 1866 was a nation dominated by the poor law, asylums, crime and the Kirk, and all would be glimpsed as I slowly reconstructed the events of that year, While being interviewed for a BBC Scotland family history radio series in 2008, the greatest surprise of all turned up regarding the aftermath of the murder, revealing a tale of bitterness and tragedy which continued for more than twenty years after Janet's death.

By pure coincidence, the BBC would also reveal yet another significant development with the story. In 2010, one of the corporation's Freedom of Information researchers, Julia Ross, made a request to every police force in the country – some fifty-two in total – to ask them to disclose how many unsolved murders they still had listed as active investigations. Only the Police Service of Northern Ireland and Gwent Police failed to respond. A total of 1,143 unsolved murder investigations were declared by the remaining forces to still be officially open. Of these, the murder of Janet Rogers was found to not only be the longest outstanding case, but also the only one still on the books from the nineteenth century.

There are some caveats to the information returned for the BBC request; the Metropolitan Police supplied figures from 1996 only, Greater Manchester from 2000, Gloucestershire from 2004, North Yorkshire from 1984 and Bedfordshire from 2000. The exercise nevertheless prompted journalist Dominic Casciani to pen an article entitled 'When the Murder Trail Goes Cold' for the BBC News website's *Magazine* section (Thursday, 6 May 2010), in which he declared the case of Janet Henderson or Rogers to be the United Kingdom's oldest unsolved murder case. Whether it is the UK's oldest unsolved murder case may certainly be open to challenge; it is most certainly the oldest unsolved case by a modern Scottish police force.

The Mount Stewart Murder has lingered in the folk memory of Forgandenny to the modern era, albeit tenuously. On my first visit to the area, in 2002, I learned of some interesting anecdotes still shared by the locals, of seemingly half-remembered tales passed down through the generations. In one example, Janet's body had apparently been discovered stuffed in a press; in another story it was said that the 'village idiot' had allegedly committed the crime. Such tales would not turn out to be true, but folk history can often be as fascinating as the truth it purports to represent.

The landscape where the murder occured had changed little across time. The small village of Forgandenny has a few more houses now than existed in 1866, but the area itself is still largely dominated by the farms mentioned in this book, including Mount Stewart Farm. Some buildings mentioned within the tale have disappeared, such as the two cottages at Linnlea which feature so prominantly, although their foundations can still be found amongst the overgrown grass now hiding their former existence from the main road, which passes by just a couple of hundred meters away. The nearby village of Bridge of Earn has perhaps changed the most, today being a major suburb for the city of Perth, located just a few miles away and now easily accessible by a motorway link that may well have been the envy of those travelling by steam, foot or cart so long ago.

From all of the material that I have gathered, I have tried to faithfully outline the detail of the murder and the subsequent investigation, largely in chronological order. As well as the story itself, I have also tried to convey a sense of some of the other contemporary events which impacted on the investigation. Most of the dialogue is based on newspaper reportage and recorded interview transcripts from precognition papers – precognition in Scotland being nothing to do with the supernatural, but rather the process of recording statements to help advocates and solicitors become aware of the evidence that will likely be made available should a case go to trial. At times, some license has been given with dialogue to help the story flow where exact conversations are not recorded, though all of it is based on the facts as identified.

I should add that I am not Taggart, and I have not tried to solve the murder. This book outlines the events as known to have happened, to explore the world of a Victorian murder investigation in rural Scotland, and to detail the consequences as established afterwards. It is, of course, also a tale that helped to shape the lives of both myself and my children, having so dramatically impacted our ancestors' lives after the horrendous events of 1866. There may be other sources concerning the story that I have yet to discover and I am only too happy to hear theories about the cause of the killing and about the identity of the murderer.

Chris Paton, 2012

ACKNOWLEDGEMENTS

My first thanks must to go to Greg Ross, who first alerted me to the true cause of Janet Rogers' death and set me in pursuit of my ancestral tale.

In January 2008, the story of the Mount Stewart Murder was featured on the BBC Radio Scotland series 'Digging Up Your Roots', and I was asked to participate. The University of Dundee Archive Service retrieved many relevant records from its collection for the recording, one of which I have kindly been granted permission to use within this work. As much to Patricia Whatley and the team there, I must also express gratitude to the BBC's Rhona Brudenell and Claire White for facilitating the opportunity.

I must also thank the truly wonderful Willie McFarlane, the honorary curator of Dundee's Tayside Police Museum. Not only did Willie provide many detailed answers to what must have seemed like a never-ending series of questions about the history of the force, his own *The History of the Perthshire and Kinross-shire Constabularies* was invaluable in helping me to understand the contemporary backdrop for the following account.

Many members of staff at the National Records of Scotland have been of great assistance during the research process, and I must thank the ever helpful Robin Urquhart and Denise Cowan for permission to reproduce certain images. Thanks must also go to Tom Dennis for permission to use an illustration which accompanied an article written by me for *Your Family Tree* magazine in 2007, and to Pamela Coventry at the Murray Royal Hospital in Perth for additional illustrative material.

Several staff members at the A.K. Bell Library in Perth were immensely helpful in securing newspaper coverage for the investigation, and particular thanks must be given to Christine Wood and Jan Merchant at Perth and Kinross Archives who helped to source many contemporary police records and letters from the investigation. Claire Sturrock, archivist at Tayside Police, was valiant in trying to locate surviving relevant material from the investigation, as was the Dunblane-based solicitor's firm Thomas and J.W. Barty. I must also express gratitude to Celia Heritage for research carried out on my behalf at the British Library's newspaper archive at Colindale, to Jayne Shrimpton for advice on contemporary clothing styles, and, of course, to The History Press for expressing an interest in a book on the subject and for waiting so patiently for its delivery. In particular, a huge thanks is also given to Matilda Richards for her skilful editing of the manuscript.

There are many to whom gratitude must be expressed who will sadly never receive it. Many people were involved in the pursuit of justice in 1866 and 1867, and as will be seen, others were affected by both the tragedy itself and its eventual outcome. In the hi-tech world of today it can be hard to imagine an investigation without the use of DNA evidence, fingerprint specialists, psychological profiling or any other techniques of forensic investigation as we might now understand them. The concept of criminal investigation officers was barely in its infancy in Scotland at this time, and there were no high-speed communications beyond the telegraph, the handbill and the steam train. The absence of such modern investigative techniques at that time does not equate to the absence of effort and, despite the eventual outcome, many good officers worked hard to try to find the killer.

To the previous generations of my family caught up in such a desperate affair, I have to offer a belated gratitude for finding their way through it. What has been an exercise in storytelling for me was of course something much more difficult for them.

Finally, my wife Claire, and sons Calum and Jamie, continue to amaze me with their tolerance of a husband and father who at times lets his obsessions with the past get in the way of the demands of the present. I hope this account of the Mount Stewart Murder will be something that my family can pass on in due course to our future descendants – as much as to my wife and sons, it is to them that this account is respectfully dedicated.

LIST OF MAIN CHARACTERS

Mount Stewart Farm, Parish of Forgandenny
William Henderson, farmer at Mount Stewart Farm
Margaret Gibson, servant
Elizabeth Bell, daughter of Margaret Gibson
Christina Miller, former servant
Janet McNab, former servant

Linnlea cottages, Parish of Forgandenny
James Crichton, ploughman
Martha Crichton or Millar, ploughman's wife
James Crichton, ploughman's son
James Barlas, mason
Jean Barlas or Hally, mason's wife
Robert Barlas, mason's son
Andrew Barlas, mason's son

Airntully, Parish of Kinclaven
Janet Rogers or Henderson, the victim
James Rogers, labourer (widower)
Ann Rogers, labourer's daughter

Merchants
Betsy Riley or McKerchar, hawker, Perth
George Kane, tobacconist, Perth
Ann Williamson or Wanton, shopkeeper, Forgandenny

James Deas, shopkeeper's son, Bridge of Earn
Robert Dewar, shopkeeper's son, Bridge of Earn
Thomas Marshall, shopkeeper, Stanley

Vicinity of Mount Stewart Farm
William Gormack, farmer, West Mill
Christine Gormack, farmer's daughter, West Mill
Archibald Harris, cattle dealer, Pitkeathly
John Ritchie, farmer, Dumbuils
Mary Ritchie or Donaldson, farmer's wife, Dumbuils
Jessie McNeil or Hutton, farm servant, Baxterknowe
Alexander McCathie, blacksmith, Glenearn

Perthshire County Constabulary
Chief Constable George Gordon, Perth
Superintendent Henry McDonald, Perth
Sergeant Charles Ross, Perth (later Inspector, New Rattray)
Constable John Cameron, Perth (later parochial officer)
Constable George Mearns, Perth (later Inspector, Perth)
Constable Robert Glass, Perth
Constable Alexander Cumming, Bridge of Earn
Constable Trevor Rowley, Forgandenny

Legal authorities
Sir George Deas, Lord Deas, Lord Commissioner of Justiciary
James Adam, Advocate Depute
James Arthur Crichton, Advocate Depute
Hugh Barclay, Sheriff Substitute, Perth
John McLean, Procurator Fiscal, Perth
John Young, Deputy Procurator Fiscal, Perth
James Barty, Procurator Fiscal, Dunblane
Melville Jameson, Procurator Fiscal, Perth
Henry Whyte, solicitor, Perth
Charles Scott, solicitor, Perth
David Smart, architect, Perth

Physicians
Dr James Laing, Bridge of Earn
Dr George Webster Absolon, Perth
Dr William Henderson, Perth

ONE

MARKET DAY

Early on the morning of Friday, 30 March 1866, fifty-year-old farmer William Henderson arose from his bed to prepare for the weekly journey to the agricultural market at Perth. He walked groggily towards the simple mahogany washstand in the corner of the room and poured some water from a white china jug into its large ceramic bowl, before lifting handfuls of the liquid to wash away the sleep from his tired eyes.

The big farmer was a typical example of his calling – at five foot eleven inches in height and with a somewhat stout but muscular frame, albeit one now growing increasingly worn with age. Throwing on the same white shirt that he had been wearing for the last week, and a pair of thick, stained corduroy trousers, the lack of a good woman's presence in the house was only too apparent. Still unmarried, despite the constant promptings of his sisters and nieces, Henderson's whole life was centred entirely on his farm; the thought of a bothersome wife getting in the way had never really appealed to him. It was not that he did not like women, of course, and far from it – it was the commitment that deeply disinterested him. Whilst that had led at times to a lonely existence, the daily toils of farm work were more than enough to keep him satisfied in his temperate life.

Fully dressed, the farmer stepped out of his downstairs bedroom into the hallway and opened the large wooden front door into the unkept front garden, carved out from the surrounding fields many years before and surrounded by a low stone wall. Standing at the doorstep of the property, he lifted his gaze to take in the view of the magnificent Ochil Hills which towered over the farm. Amid the chill of the fresh spring air the early morning sun had cast a deep orange light on the huge hills before him, making every ripple in the landscape stand out vibrantly against the cloudless blue sky.

Henderson's home was Mount Stewart Farm, situated within the parish of Forgandenny, at the very end of the beautiful Perthshire valley of Strathearn. Previously known as 'The Fluars' over half a century before, the old and dilapidated two-storey building had recently been renewed to a degree by the farmer, with one half extended and a slate roof added to replace the previous thatch. The house was tucked in snugly behind a small hill facing onto the main road connecting Forgandenny and Dunning, and was further hidden from many neighbouring steadings to the north by a screen of tall trees. To the east was Pitkeathly Wells, famed throughout Scotland for the supposed healing properties of its waters; to the west lay the two farms of North and South Dumbuils. Access to Mount Stewart was only possible by a steep track which hugged the east side of the hill and worked its way down to the road. As a consequence, visitors tended to be few and far between, giving the farmer the illusion at times of living in splendid isolation.

Like so many others in the area, William Henderson was a proud tenant farmer working his land under a nineteen-year lease granted to him by Lord Ruthven of the vast Freeland estate. The Ruthven family was one of two great dynasties which had dominated the area around Forgandenny for several centuries; the other was the Oliphant family. Between them, these two noble families had shaped the local environment, and still controlled much of the parochial economy.

The small village of Forgandenny, less than a mile up the road, had been built by the Ruthven family many years before to accommodate the labourers working on the estate. In the late eighteenth century, the agricultural revolution which had been rapidly transforming the traditional farming practices of lowland Scotland had also come to lower Strathearn. Taking note of the new farming practices to the south of the country and in England, the great estate owners had dissected the lower fertile plains of the parish into a series of much smaller steadings which could then be controlled by an emergent class of tenant farmers with long-term leases. With security of tenure, this encouraged them to be entrepreneurial and to see through any proposed schemes which might increase the yield of their crops. The improvements had been successful and the land now yielded considerably more crops and wealth than in the previous century.

Before becoming a farmer, William Henderson had grown up as a child much further north in Airntully, a small village within the parish of Kinclaven, historically home to a community of handloom weavers. His parents, Andrew Henderson and Janet McEwan, had married in March 1809, and had successfully raised a family of four. Born in 1813, William was the second eldest of the children, with his sister Janet just over two years older than him. By the late 1830s the household had started to see major changes, with the three daughters soon growing up and leaving the fold. In the 1841 census, only an unmarried William was recorded as still being resident at the family home alongside his parents and a couple of farm servants. When his mother had died of heart disease just a couple of years later, both William and his devastated father had reluctantly taken the decision to uproot from their long-established home to seek an opportunity elsewhere.

Mount Stewart was one of several farm leases on the Freeland estate advertised in the Perthshire newspapers throughout March and April of 1845. With its fifty-four acres of arable land and a further ten of pasture, the two Henderson men had found the idea of managing the property to be an attractive proposition. They applied to take over the concern from the term day of Martinmas, on 11 November, and were successful.

From the outset the two men had had much to do. The advertisement had suggested that the land was still capable of much improvement – in reality this had turned out to be a precondition for the acceptance of the tenancy. Two years prior to their arrival a huge drainage project had already been started on the Freeland estate. Long furrows were being dug out of the marshy soil and then filled with drainage tiles, through which excess water could be returned to the water table. This further increased the quality of the soil, and therefore the available acreage for crop growth. The Hendersons had enjoyed such a challenge.

As the land improved, father and son had eagerly set about raising new crops, rotating oats and barley annually with root vegetables such as turnips. Potatoes for the London markets were another important production, having become popular in Strathearn since their introduction to the area at the beginning of the century, where they had originally been grown as a staple food for French prisoners of war held in the nearby city of Perth. On top of this was the raising of livestock, primarily cattle and some pigs. Such a range of work could not be carried out by the two men alone, and so several agricultural labourers were employed seasonally to help work the farm, whilst a domestic servant provided their meals and did the cleaning. For several years, their efforts had generated impressive results, and life had once again become good for the two Henderson men.

And then Andrew had suddenly died. The death of his father in April 1851 from influenza had been a blow that William Henderson had never really recovered from, the shock of it still cutting deep within him. Upon his father's death, he inherited assets valued at over £164, and the lease was reconfirmed solely in his name. Although he would be financially comfortable in the forthcoming years, from that point on the farmer had nobody but himself to rely on at Mount Stewart.

The fresh air having fully awakened him, Henderson now walked through the small garden gate and along a path up the west side of the building towards the rear of the property. Crossing a muddy courtyard, he soon reached the complex of outbuildings which contained the cattle court and cart shed, as well as the stables which housed his three horses. The farmer entered the straw-filled byre inside and checked on the condition of a heavily pregnant cow that was resting in the corner. Although due to give birth at any stage in the next few days, the animal was quite comfortable. Stepping back outside, he passed the empty piggery, and filled a bucket of water from the well to give to the cow, the muscles in his arm and back aching as he turned the handle to bring up the water from the bottom. In days gone by, this would have been one of the labourers' jobs, but times had changed over the last fifteen years.

The strain of the business had greatly taken its toll on Henderson. For the last four months, life had been particularly hard within the Perthshire farming community. The county was currently in the midst of a deadly cattle plague epidemic, a blight that had already ravaged much of Britain following its arrival to her shores in the previous year. The rinderpest plague had first arrived in London in July 1865, its source attributed to the import of cattle to the Islington market from Holland and Belgium. Its timing could not have been worse, with the threatened return of cholera making itself felt in the English capital also, and the cost of meat already at a high premium. Within the first month of its detection, over 2,000 animals had been slaughtered in London to try to prevent the spread of the infection. It was a desperate ploy which failed, with many diseased animals having already made their way across the country in railway trucks and by sea up the coast.

The first case in Scotland had been discovered in the Borders town of Kelso in the first week of August, with some fourteen cattle afflicted. Those that survived were sent back to London, but the plague would not be so easily contained, spreading rapidly across the country. Soon Edinburgh was hit, and then the north of the country. In one case a farmer was reported to have paid £20 for an animal which had shown no signs of the malady; hours later it had died. By the end of 1865, more than 3,000 Scottish farms had been hit, and over 40,000 cattle infected, with most either dying of the plague or being slaughtered to prevent its further spread.

Perthshire had initially remained immune to its advances, managing to stave off the pestilence until the end of October. At this point an outbreak had then occurred at the Carse of Gowrie, followed a few days later within the city of Perth itself. To try and prevent further contact with the disease, a series of control orders had been imposed upon the county's farmers since January of the present year, to prevent the movement of livestock without a license. In the north of the county, many had initially chosen rather foolishly to ignore this measure; whole herds were soon slaughtered in consequence of their inaction.

Mercifully the parish of Forgandenny was as yet unaffected, but Henderson knew that it would only be a matter of time before the plague breached its meagre defences. Even the Presbyterian churches in the parish had weighed in to do their best to help. On the previous day, a Fast Day had been held, with local kirks of both the main denominations requiring their congregations to attend church and pray for repentance over the supposed misdemeanour that had led to the epidemic. Henderson had not gone, perhaps suspecting that if God had chosen for the country to suffer such pestilence, he might well have had his reasons.

Walking from the byre towards the kitchen, the farmer turned the handle on the door and stepped inside to find his sister, Janet, stirring a large pot of porridge over the fire. He grunted a good morning as he sat down at a large rounded oak table in the corner of the room, on which were laid a couple of porcelain bowls and spoons for the breakfast she was about to share with him.

Janet was not a resident of Mount Stewart Farm, but had come to stay temporarily to help her younger brother out. Her usual residence continued to be within the village of Airntully, where she and William had been raised as children. For thirty years she had been married to James Rogers, a labourer who worked regularly away from home on some of the more prosperous estates to the north of Perth. With her husband she had raised five healthy daughters, with only the two youngest, Ann and Mary, still living at home. Both girls had for many years worked a six-day week as weavers in the neighbouring factory town of Stanley, but a swelling that had recently been detected on Ann's brain had begun to seriously affect her eyesight, to the point where she had been forced to give up her job. Two other daughters, Catherine and Margaret, also resided close by, working in the vicinity as domestic servants. The couple's eldest daughter, twenty-eight-year-old Janet, had left home eight years previously after her marriage to a Perth-born currier, William Hay Paton. She now lived in Blackford, with her husband and three young sons, making her mother and father very proud grandparents.

Earlier that week, on the Monday, Henderson had travelled north to Airntully by cart to ask for Janet's help at the farm. His servant had just left his employment on the previous Thursday and he wondered if she might allow his niece Mary to come to Mount Stewart for a couple of weeks – there was an expectant cow on the farm and he could do with some assistance until a reliable replacement could be found.

'It will be better if I come down,' Janet had suggested. 'In any case, who knows how to pull a calf out better?' It was true, for she had often helped their father when it had come to calving at some of the local farms within the parish of Kinclaven. Henderson was grateful for the offer, but was then a little disappointed to discover that his sister would not travel back with him that day. It was therefore decided that he would pick her up at the railway station in Perth a couple of days later on the Wednesday. It was now Friday, and having had time to settle in, Janet was today intending to make a start with the cleaning whilst her brother was at the market.

The breakfast now ready, Janet joined her brother at the table to eat. During their meal, they discussed their respective plans for the day. Henderson would be shortly setting off for Perth to buy some provisions and fertiliser, and intended to look at the pigs that were for sale at the market. He also needed to pick up some slates at the neighbouring village of Bridge of Earn, or 'the Brig' as it was known locally, for repairs that were to be made to the roofs of his outbuildings on the following Saturday. As such, he envisaged being away for most of the day.

Janet noticed that her brother had no whitening with which she could clean the house. After chastising him for the state of the place, she asked him to pick up a quantity whilst he was out. In the meantime, she would spend the day bringing some general order back to the property, and would tend to the animals.

'Mind,' she added, 'I may have to drop everything and take the train into Perth, should Uncle William send a note.' Before leaving the station on Wednesday, Janet had posted a message to their revered uncle, Dr William Henderson of Perth, to ask if she could visit him. Both siblings were fond of their uncle, a truly remarkable pioneer in the field of medicine, and the family's greatest success story. Among his many achievements, he had in 1820 performed one of the country's earliest successful caesarean operations in Perth, when both Janet and William had still been young children; the resultant baby had been duly christened 'Caesar Anna' in honour of the occasion. The development of a 'stomachic elixir' medicine had also earned him a considerable fortune and reputation, and at eighty-two years of age he was a widely respected elder with the East Church of Perth. The younger William Henderson regularly dined with his uncle on his weekly forays into the city, though on this day would have to forego such a meeting in order to fetch his slates.

With breakfast completed, Janet cleared away the dishes, whilst her brother went outside to prepare for his trip ahead. The farmer's immediate priority was to now inform his ploughman of the work he wished to be completed in his absence. Observing his servant in the field to the east of the farm, he crossed over to address him.

James Crichton was a forty-four-year-old labourer from Portmoak in Fife, and had been hired by Henderson for a six-month term from Martinmas of the previous year. At five feet and six inches in height, he was of average build, with fair complexion and a bushy unkempt beard. After accepting the contract to work at Mount Stewart he had moved with his wife and two youngest children to reside at the nearby cottages of Linnlea, conveniently located some 500 yards down the hill from the farmhouse, just off the track leading to the main Forgandenny road. Crichton was a good worker, but Henderson's relationship with his employee had become immensely strained of late.

The problems between the two men had started earlier in the year. On the last Friday of January, Henderson had taken his servant to Perth to help him with a delivery of grain, the pair having left Mount Stewart at eight o'clock in the morning. The delivery had been made within a couple of hours and the farmer had then instructed Crichton to take the cart back to the farm, while he remained in the city to attend to additional business.

Henderson had not returned home until later in the evening. With only the dying light of the gloaming to illuminate his way back, he had entered his farmhouse and progressed through the darkened interior towards his bedroom, in order to place some money into a chest. Walking past the window he had suddenly felt the sensation of glass cracking under his feet. An examination of the window found that two panes had been smashed and the frame damaged. Some villain had clearly gained entry to the house. Startled, the farmer had immediately searched the room and had soon discovered that the chest within which he usually kept his money had been forced open. A purse containing £1 in silver coins was found to be missing, as well as a further sum of £2 in coins wrapped up in separate pieces of paper. A silver watch and Albert chain were also found to have been stolen, in addition to a pair of worsted cord trousers.

On the following morning the farmer had reported the incident to Thomas Rowley, the local police constable from Forgandenny, and then to his ploughman. Crichton had suggested that any marks made by the intruder's feet might still have been visible in the soil beneath the window. The two men searched unsuccessfully for such marks, but it was obvious that the soil had been turned over by somebody covering his tracks, with a small flowerpot dragged over to clumsily half cover the spot. With such a targeted suggestion, Henderson had immediately suspected Crichton of having committed the offence, he having had ample opportunity to do so during his master's absence in Perth. There was no evidence to prove such an allegation and the farmer had therefore held his tongue.

About a week after the burglary, Henderson had received word that one of Crichton's sons had found the pair of missing trousers which had been stolen from his house. He confirmed that the trousers were indeed his, and was informed by his ploughman that they had been discovered in a small wood behind the law of Dumbuils to the west of the farm. The farmer's suspicions were further raised by this revelation, he having walked through the wood himself on a couple of occasions that week. There was still no proof that his servant was lying, but Henderson no longer trusted him. In the weeks that followed, their relationship deteriorated considerably.

As soon as he reached the labourer, Henderson informed Crichton that when he was finished with his current ploughing task, he was to move a quantity of nitrate of soda from one of the storage sheds. Once completed, he was to then remove some fence posts on the head-ridge between two of the fields, and to plough the area. As the farmer was planning on going to Perth by cart, he also informed Crichton that he would only be able to use two of the horses to help him with his tasks. The ploughman grunted his understanding and, turning his back on his master, continued to work the plough as before.

The big farmer returned to the farmhouse and stepped into his bedroom to fetch some money from a small chest hidden inside a press beside the large window. After removing enough to pay for a pig and the much needed provisions, he grabbed his cap and jacket from the stand in the hallway and once again exited the house. Crossing over to the cart shed, he wheeled the cart out to the main courtyard before fetching one of the horses from the stable and hooking it up to the harness. A heavily tarnished brass plate was affixed to the back of the cart, and using his sleeve Henderson gave it a quick clean to reveal his surname inscribed upon it.

At a few minutes before ten o'clock he called into the kitchen that he was about to set off. Janet's head appeared around the door. 'Have a good day at the market and I'll see you this evening,' she shouted, followed by a final, 'Mind the whitening!'

Henderson climbed up onto the front of the cart and, after donning his hat, picked up the reins and called to the horse to walk on.

——·——

The city of Perth was approximately five miles north of Mount Stewart. The harsh frosts and snows of the recent winter months had finally gone, and the warm spring sun was managing to make fleeting appearances from behind a scattering of ever thickening cumulus clouds. A slight breeze also made the journey somewhat more comfortable for both the farmer and his horse as they trundled slowly along the country lanes towards the Bridge of Earn. On reaching the village, Henderson coaxed the horse to take him over the bridge towards the north side of the River Earn, famous as far afield as London for its wild salmon. Following the road between Kirkton Hill and Moncreiffe Hill, he made his way into Perth through the city's South Inch, where Oliver Cromwell had once built a citadel some two centuries before. From here he proceeded further north into the southern suburbs of the city itself.

There were two main markets held every week in Perth, on Wednesdays and Fridays, with that on Friday being the principle event. At these gatherings, the farmers of the neighbourhood would meet at the cross to give and receive intelligence on a whole range of relevant subjects, from the state of current prices to any other matter that might affect the agricultural interests of the county's gentlemen. Friday was also the day when butter, eggs and other necessities were brought in for sale, and when provisions would be purchased for the week ahead.

Henderson pulled up at the market, disembarked from his cart and secured his horse. The farmer's main requirement today was to buy a supply of guano, a commonly used fertiliser made from the droppings of birds, which was particularly high in phosphorus and nitrogen. Before looking for the fertiliser, he first made his way to an auction, where, after viewing several of the beasts for sale, he purchased a stout-looking pig. Changing his mind about the guano, he instead purchased a smaller amount of nitrate of soda and hauled it onto the back of his vehicle.

The farmer then made his way to his favoured cart stop of Logiealmond Tavern on Methven Street, where he proceeded to catch up on all the latest gossip and information relevant to his vocation. The big news was of course the cattle plague, with a couple of cases brought to the attention of the local justices of the peace during the last week. On Monday, a farmer called Donald McCallum had fallen foul of the County Constabulary for having driven forty-nine sheep to Forteviot railway station from Glenlyon without a movement license. It had apparently been a simple misunderstanding. McCallum had thought that a previous license covering the movement of some eight hundred of his stock had also covered this smaller group, comprised of the weaker of his animals, which had had to be moved on a separate occasion.

On the following day, a farm servant called John Buchanan had then been discovered transporting two cartloads of hay between the Bridge of Earn and Dunning on behalf of his master, a Stirling-based dealer. Unfortunately for him, the hay was being moved under a license granted in Stirling which was invalid in Perthshire. The movement of the carts had been stopped by the local constable until the necessary paperwork had been arranged. Both had been relatively minor indiscretions, but the farmers understood the importance of complying fully with the law, knowing that at any moment their continued livelihoods might very well depend on it.

By five o'clock daylight had started to fade. After making his farewells at the tavern, Henderson once again climbed up onto his cart, and with the reins of his horse in hand started his journey back home. Just after six o'clock he reached the Bridge of Earn and stopped at the grocery shop of James Deas to buy the whitening required by his sister. From there he moved on to the house of John Geddes, the village slater. Although he was due to work at the farm on Saturday, Geddes informed the farmer that owing to a change of his circumstances the earliest he could now make it would be the following Monday, to which Henderson reluctantly agreed. After loading the cart with some slates for the job ahead, he bid the slater goodnight and once more resumed his travels home.

It was now almost dark. With only the twilight to guide him, Henderson made his way cautiously along the tree-lined stretch of road back towards Forgandenny. He passed a few small houses along the way – the dwellings at Ballendrick, Pitkeathly Villas and the cottages at Carmichael – and glimpsed the occasional flicker of a domestic fire through an open window. Just before seven o'clock he reached Orchard Seat, at which point he took a left turn onto the narrow lane leading towards his farm. The horse strained to pull the cart up the hill, passing the two cottages at Linnlea to the left, and within a couple of minutes had entered the courtyard at Mount Stewart.

As Henderson called on the horse to stop, he noticed with satisfaction from the long ridges in the field to the west of the house that his ploughman had made considerable progress. From the noise in the stables he deduced that Crichton was putting his own horses away for the night after his day's work. The farmer called over to the labourer to help with offloading the pig from the back of the cart and to then put it into the empty piggery beside the cattle court. This done, he further instructed Crichton to remove the fertiliser and slates from the cart, while he removed the harness from his own horse and led it into the stable.

With the cart placed in its shed and the horses now under cover for the night, Henderson locked the stable door and removed both the keys from the nail on the outer door post on which they hung. He crossed over to check that the pig was secure, before making his way back over the yard towards the farmhouse. As he turned the handle of the kitchen door, he was surprised to find that it was locked. Expecting his sister to be inside, he rapped hard on the window with his knuckles and called out her name.

'Janet, can ye open the door?'

There was no answer. He tried to peer through the window, but the room was too dark inside to make out whether it was inhabited or not.

'C'mon lass,' he shouted, 'it's fair cauld out here! Janet? Where are ye woman?'

Again there was no response. Where was his sister? The farmer turned to ask Crichton if he had seen her, then realised that the surly labourer had already departed down the track towards his home, his work for the day now completed. Henderson decided to try the lesser-used entrance to the house on its south-facing side – perhaps his sister was not well, and had gone to bed early? He climbed over the low stone wall into the garden and tested the handle on the large wooden door, only to discover that this too was locked.

The farmer set off after his servant in the hope that he might know where his sister was. Reaching Linnlea a few minutes later, Henderson knocked on the half open front door of Crichton's small cottage, before stepping inside to ask the ploughman if he had seen his sister. The surprised labourer answered that he had not known she was his sister, but he had briefly glimpsed her talking to a man at the back door at about eleven o'clock. He had not seen her since, having spent the afternoon ploughing the field as instructed. Considering the possibility that Janet may have received word from their uncle in Perth, Henderson further enquired as to whether his employee had seen anybody approach the farm during the day, to which the answer was an abrupt no. Bidding his servant's wife goodnight, the farmer stepped back out of the cottage and made his way back up the hill towards the house.

It was clear that with both of the doors locked the only way to try to effect entry would be through an upstairs window. Fetching a ladder from the milk shed, Henderson propped it up on the east-facing side of the house beside his sister's bedroom window, which he hoped would be unfastened. With great care he climbed slowly up, careful not to lose his balance as he did so. Reaching the top, he peered through the window and tried calling out Janet's name, louder this time; the response was the same that had greeted his earlier efforts. The farmer tried to lift the heavy window in the frame and was relieved to find that the lock was unlatched. After pushing it up as far as it would go, he carefully squeezed himself through the narrow gap it afforded and into the bedroom.

Once inside, he carefully stepped towards the bed in the low light, being careful not to awaken his sister who he hoped would be asleep there. It was soon clear that Janet was not present. Henderson made his way slowly to the bedroom door and out towards the landing. Thinking that perhaps his sister might have instead taken to sleeping in his bedroom, he walked cautiously down the creaky, wooden staircase to the ground floor, and quietly stepped into his room. Once again he found that it was empty.

By now the farmer was convinced that, for whatever reason, Janet was most certainly not in the house. Possibly she had received a message from Perth after all and had been unable to inform Crichton or his wife of her sudden change in plans? If so, she would at least be safe for the night at their uncle's splendid Georgian house in the city's Rose Terrace, and would no doubt be back again early on the following day. At this point, the possibility suddenly occurred to the farmer that Janet might in fact be asleep in the servant's box bed in the corner of the kitchen. Keeping the hallway wall to his left, he fumbled his way towards the interior door of the kitchen and pushed it open.

As with the rest of the house, the room was almost pitch black, with a couple of dying embers on the fire too far gone to cast any useful illumination. The only light available was that from the now rising moon reflected off the white frame of the kitchen's single window. Henderson was surprised to notice a strong smell of eggs emanating from within the darkness, and considered that it was perhaps the remains of a snack that Janet had eaten earlier.

The farmer walked to the back door of the house, hoping to open it to provide a little more light into the room, in order that he might find a candle. He moved his hand down towards the lock to turn the key and was surprised to discover that it was not there. This was extremely unusual, as only Crichton and he ever took possession of the big iron key when it was not in the door. The labourer had certainly not mentioned having taken it.

As he moved back into the kitchen once more, Henderson's foot collided with something solid on the floor. Startled, he bent down to see what had been struck, and discovered that it was one of the wooden chairs in the room, which was lying on its back. He lifted it up and set it back against the wall.

The farmer's eyes were finally beginning to adjust to the gloomy interior. He could now make out the form of another chair that was on its side in front of the dresser in the far corner, whilst between the fire and the window a large pile of clothing seemed to have been dumped unceremoniously on the floor.

The hairs on the back of Henderson's neck slowly began to rise – something was not right. Crichton had evidently expected Janet to be in the house. If his sister had somehow walked past his house unnoticed and had indeed gone to Perth, why would she have taken the kitchen key with her and not left it with him or a member of his family?

As he stepped closer to the pile of clothing Henderson realised that it was actually comprised of sheets and blankets that had been dragged across the length of the room from the small box bed in the opposite corner. Approaching to investigate, he was surprised to feel his foot splashing into a small puddle on the floor beside the unruly heap. He lifted the top sheet back and immediately gasped in horror – a pale white hand was outstretched before him, opened wide but unmoving.

Dropping the sheet, he stood back in shock. Dear God, it could not be. Stooping down once more, he pulled the sheet back further. Staring at him from beneath the covers was his sister's expressionless face, her eyes open, gazing emptily back towards his own.

Panicking, the farmer took hold of his sister's hand, to find that it contained no warmth, and that her arm was rigid. He realised that the coarse woollen blanket covering her was also wet, smeared with a sticky liquid which he now deduced from the pungent smell was blood. In the limited light, he could just make out that his sister's hair was wet; the two woollen caps covering the back of her head were soaked in blood also.

The awful truth was only too apparent. Janet Rogers, his sister, had been brutally murdered.

TWO

MURDER AT MOUNT STEWART

William Henderson was in complete shock, a thousand questions working their way through his grief-stricken mind. The fact of his sister's murder was as incomprehensible to him as it was gruesome. Who could have killed Janet in such a brutal manner, and for what possible motivation? Had she struggled with her unknown assailant, or had she mercifully not known of the killer's presence and been struck down dead by his first blow? They were desperate questions, with no obvious answers.

Having found Janet's body in such distressing circumstances, he unlocked the front door and hurriedly left the house to fetch help from Barlas, who lived in the cottage next door to James Crichton at Linnlea. As he had done at his servant's house half an hour earlier, he knocked loudly on the mason's door and stepped inside, to find that Barlas, his family and two sons were eating a late supper. The mason had not long returned from a full day's work at the new railway tunnel currently under construction at Moncreiffe Hill, which overlooked the Bridge of Earn. 'Jamie, Jamie,' the farmer cried out in anguish. 'Come awa' up, for my sister is either dead or murdered.' He described the horrific scene he had just discovered at the farmhouse, and desperately implored the mason to come and see for himself. A surprised Barlas agreed and, leaving his boys to finish their meal, soon exited the cottage with his wife and the distraught farmer.

Upon reaching the farmhouse, Barlas at first asked Henderson if he was quite sure that his sister was dead. William stooped down to lift back the blanket covering her face. 'The evidence speaks for itself,' he replied.

Discussing what to do next, the two men made their way outside to the garden. At the gate they found Crichton talking to Barlas's wife. It transpired that whilst the three adults had walked up to the farm, the mason's thirteen-year-old son, Andrew, had gone excitedly to his neighbour's door to inform him of what was happening. Although Crichton and his master did not get along, the labourer claimed that he had felt an obligation to see whether he could help.

Ignoring Henderson, Crichton asked Barlas what was happening, to which the mason replied that his master's sister had been brutally murdered some time that day. Glancing suspiciously at the farmer, Crichton suggested that if that was the case, the police should be summoned to the scene at once – he would go and inform Constable Rowley from Forgandenny, he stated, at which point he left the assembled group and set off for the village. Barlas suggested to Henderson that he should fetch both the doctor and the constable from the Bridge of Earn. The farmer agreed, but on asking the mason to accompany him, Barlas's wife stated that she was too distressed to be left on her own; her husband would have to remain behind.

In daylight, the journey to 'the Brig' was ordinarily a fifteen-minute walk along the tree-lined main road, but that evening Henderson moved as quickly as he could, half walking and half running. By the light of a barely visible moon he once more passed Mrs Williamson's grocery shop at Carmichael Cottages, and then the cottages of Pitkeathly and Dunbarney Villas. Upon reaching the railway track he crossed over and made his way hastily into the south of the village.

Walking swiftly down Front Street towards the Gas Light Company complex at Sealsbridge, which supplied the area with fuel for domestic lighting, Henderson finally reached the home of the village physician, Dr Laing. A heavy rap on the door quickly brought the doctor's wife, Agnes, to enquire as to the nature of his business at such a late time in the evening. The farmer blurted out the urgency of the situation, at which point the appalled woman informed him that her husband was not in, as he had gone to Edinburgh for the day. He was expected to arrive back shortly; a carriage was waiting to collect him at the railway station.

Henderson thanked the woman and then made his way towards the village police station, a small semi-detached cottage at Sealsbank, located about 300 yards from the train station. The building was manned by thirty-one-year-old Constable Alexander Cumming, a recent newcomer who had been posted to the station just a year before. Henderson soon apprised the policeman of his gruesome discovery, and, after grabbing a heavy glazed coat from a stand, the constable accompanied the farmer to meet the train.

Reaching the station building, Henderson and Constable Cumming made their way towards the ticket office, where they found the stationmaster preparing for the arrival of the last Perth-bound train of the day. After explaining the nature of their emergency, the constable asked for some paper with which to write a note. The stationmaster duly obliged, handing him a sheet of company memorandum paper, on which Henderson urgently scribbled down the following plea to the procurator fiscal in Perth:

Dear Sir,
Please come out here as soon as possible as my sister has been murdered today while I was in Perth.
Your obdt sert,
Wm. Henderson

With the note placed into an envelope by Cumming and suitably addressed, the constable then stepped out onto the station to find a potential carrier. A middle-aged lady of the constable's acquaintance, seated on a bench outside, readily agreed to convey the note as urgently as possible to the fiscal's office within County Buildings on the city's South Street.

The sound of a whistle alerted the party to the imminent arrival of the 9.20 p.m. North British Rail train to Perth. The huge engine slowly came into view in the distance, a thick plume of white steam bellowing out of its single chimney and dissipating into the darkness above. As the train crawled purposefully along the track towards the station, a long, piercing screech of the brakes suddenly filled the air as the engine pulled up alongside the platform to deliver its passengers from Edinburgh. With the train coming to a halt, the doors of its three carriages opened, and onto the platform stepped the imposing figure of Dr James Laing, to be greeted by Cumming and Henderson. Convinced of the urgent need for his skills at Mount Stewart, he took the two gentlemen to his waiting carriage and instructed the driver to take them with utmost haste to the scene of the tragedy.

On their arrival at the farm the party was greeted in the yard by Constable Thomas Rowley, the fifty-four-year-old Irish-born constable of Forgandenny having already been summonsed by Crichton not long before. Rowley led his constabulary colleague and the doctor through the door to the rear of the property and into the kitchen, which was now lit by a single candle. A quick examination by Dr Laing followed, which, to the farmer's distress, confirmed that his sister was most certainly dead.

After debating the immediate priorities in such a situation, the two constables concluded that there was little that they could do but secure the site until the arrival of the procurator fiscal and his party from Perth. Both men also realised that they would need more illumination, as it would be a long night ahead of them. Getting little response from the shocked farmer,

Crichton was directed to accompany Rowley to fetch some candles and a few coals from Mrs Williamson's shop at Carmichael Cottages on the main road below.

Midnight came and went. The assembled party at Mount Stewart Farm waited in silence for the authorities to arrive from Perth. Finally, at twenty minutes to one on Saturday morning, a carriage pulled up in the courtyard. Several police officers from the Perthshire County Constabulary stepped from the vehicle, followed by Superintendent Henry McDonald, the deputy chief constable, and John Young, the deputy procurator fiscal.

The investigation could now begin.

——·——

Henry McDonald gently rubbed his tired eyes as he lifted the small brass watch from his pocket to take note of the time. Scribbling with a stubby pencil into his notebook that it had just passed a quarter to one, he duly replaced his trusted timepiece and turned to inspect the gruesome scene that had demanded his attention so early in the morning.

The big fifty-one-year-old policeman was, like Constable Rowley, a native of Ireland, but had joined the Perthshire Constabulary many years earlier in 1840, making him its longest-serving member. Having started his career on the Perth Bridge beat, he had been given the position of Orderly Constable at the constabulary's original Marshall Place headquarters in the city, before rising through the ranks to his present position. Over the last quarter of a century he had witnessed many remarkable changes, both within the police and within the society he had sworn to protect.

The Perthshire County Constabulary had first been established in September 1839, with McDonald one of its earliest recruits. Under the first chief constable, Captain Joseph Grove, the Irishman had served as one of just thirty-three men responsible for policing an area well over one and a half million acres in size. In 1855, Grove had finally resigned, to be replaced by the current chief constable, George Gordon. A major new piece of legislation in 1857, the Police (Scotland) Act, had then led to a dramatic reorganisation of the force. It was now fully professionalised and had almost doubled in size, with some fifty-five officers currently serving the county's needs. McDonald had encountered many tragedies in his long and illustrious career, but this would soon rank as one of the most infamous.

Accompanying the superintendent was one of the force's two criminal officers, Sergeant Charles Ross. The idea of having criminal investigation officers within the force had only been adopted two years earlier, the role of the criminal officer having previously been under the purview of the procurator fiscal. The five foot-tall Ross-shire man, with his grey hair and ruddy complexion, had been an obvious candidate, having worked for the force for almost sixteen years. By contrast, the other criminal officer was Constable John Cameron, a twenty-six-year-old Inverness man who had only joined the constabulary less than four years before. Although part of the force, Cameron was based within the fiscal's office, acting as a point of continuity between the methods of the old regime and the new progressive methods being slowly adopted by other forces across the country.

In most cases it was usual practice for the police to investigate a crime before alerting the procurator fiscal, but murder was one of the few exceptions. In such a situation the fiscal would accompany the investigating team from the outset to direct their efforts. Fulfilling the position for Perthshire was John McLean. His role was to determine on behalf of the sheriff whether a crime had been committed, and if so, to then present the case for prosecution at the courts if a suspect could be identified and charged. In serious cases, such as murder, the fiscal would not directly prosecute the case himself, but would instead present the evidence to the Crown Office and the Lord Advocate, the chief public prosecutor for Scotland, who would then be responsible for facilitating the trial.

Earlier on the morning of Friday, 30 March, McLean had been urgently summonsed to Pitlochry in the north of the county in relation to another violent incident. His deputy assistant, John Young, had therefore been left to handle affairs on his behalf in Perth. It was Young who had received William Henderson's note just a few hours before, and who had summonsed the superintendent and his men to travel immediately to the farm. That a crime had been committed at Mount Stewart Farm was certain – it was now the duty of the police and the fiscal's office to together discover the identity of the perpetrator and the motive.

McDonald and Young had soon established that William Henderson, James Crichton and James Barlas had all been at the farmhouse upon the initial discovery of the victim's body. The deputy fiscal had instructed McDonald to have all three men formally detained in the parlour adjacent to the kitchen until the initial enquiries were completed. With the house's occupants now secured, the superintendent turned his attention to the crime scene in the kitchen.

'Dear Lord,' he proclaimed in front of the gathered party. 'The poor lass.'

'Aye, sir,' replied Sergeant Ross, 'she is that.'

With the stone walls of the room now illuminated by the flickering light of several candles, McDonald stooped down beside the fireplace to talk to the physician, Dr Laing, who was again examining the corpse of the unfortunate victim.

'The woman's body appears to be still quite warm,' observed the doctor, noting the slight temperature of the trunk against his hand, before pulling the sheet back over. Removing a small blue ribbon from her face, the doctor then pointed towards a deep, perforated wound leading from the cheek to the base of the ear.

'If you bring the candle just a bit closer to the ear, you'll see a heavy contusion just beneath the lobe. Caused, I would say, by the impact of something heavy being struck against this woman's head, and not by her fall.' Pointing to the two bloodstained woollen caps at the back of her head, he said, 'It looks as if her injuries might continue to the back of the skull – however, I do not wish to disturb the body any further without a warrant.'

As the stench of the bloody wounds began to stick in the policeman's throat, he withdrew the candle and took a step back.

'Can you hazard a guess as to the time of death, Doctor?' he enquired.

Laing stood up and faced the superintendent. 'Well it is quite cold, which may exaggerate the feel on my hand of any heat retained. My best guess at present would be at some stage in the afternoon, perhaps early in the evening.' He then directed the superintendent's gaze towards the white plaster-coated wall beside the fireplace. 'I took the liberty of making a quick examination of the room earlier, Mr McDonald. I believe that you should take a look at this.'

Leaning against the wall was a simple household kitchen axe, about a foot in length. Without displacing it from its position, McDonald gently handled the instrument and noticed that its blunted blade was also covered in congealed blood, with several long wisps of hair hanging from the edge.

'Undoubtedly the murder weapon,' he noted.

Laing concurred. 'It would seem so. A tool such as this could easily have caused such wounds.'

'The blood is still somewhat moist,' observed Ross, as he touched the surface of the blade.

'Indeed, sergeant,' answered the physician. 'I would expect that if the attack had happened earlier in the day, it would most certainly have been dried by now, but as you can see, that is not the case.'

Leaning the axe back in situ against the wall, McDonald looked at the doctor.

'Thank you for your observations, Doctor. I believe we should leave the body as it is for the moment, until we have had a chance to make a complete inventory of the scene.'

Removing a handkerchief from his pocket, he gave his hand a quick wipe where a spot of blood had made contact. 'Once we have secured a warrant from Perth, I would be further grateful if you could carry out the necessary examination. Until then, perhaps you would be so kind as to wait in the room next door with the others?'

With the doctor escorted from the room by Constable Cumming, the superintendent and his sergeant then commenced an inspection of the kitchen, starting with the fireplace. On the long-extinguished embers there was a boiler filled to half capacity with about two quarts of water, while towards the back of the fire, the remains of a cooked egg could be observed. McDonald realised that fragments of eggshells were also scattered around him on the cold stone floor.

The victim's body was lying in a large pool of dark viscous blood, which had evidently been disturbed by the feet of the killer; bloody scraped foot imprints were clearly visible on the main flagstone before the fire. The force of the blows that had rained down on the farmer's sister had been powerful enough to bespatter many items around the room with the dark liquid, with many of the still wet drops glinting in harmony with every flicker of the candlelight.

Moving towards the box bed in the corner of the room opposite the body, Sergeant Ross noted a pair of women's boots on the floor, also covered in blood. These had either been removed from the corpse after death or perhaps lifted by the killer for some reason and then discarded. The carpet cover on the box bed had been cast aside. The lid itself was open, and the woollen blankets within had been dragged out and thrown over the body. Apart from the blanket immediately covering the victim's head, the policeman noted that the rest of the bedding items were clean. The bed itself was untouched by blood.

On the floor between the bed and the body was a long bolster pillow. Lifting it up, McDonald was surprised to discover that it concealed a small, dirty clay pipe, broken into seven pieces of various sizes, as well as a small dented tin top for a pipe. The policeman made a mental note to ask Henderson whether he or his sister smoked, or if any of his previous servants had partaken of the habit. If not, the items may belong to the killer, perhaps dropped by him in his hurry to escape.

The superintendent then looked at the rest of the kitchen, casting his gaze away from the fire towards the window. It was clear that the room had been ransacked, though whether this had happened before or after the murder could not as yet be deduced. A chair was overturned and several drawers removed from a side cupboard, giving the impression that the killer had been searching earnestly for something. Both McDonald and

Ross were experienced enough to know that this may not necessarily have been the case.

McDonald called for the two constables who had been first on the scene. Turning first towards Alexander Cumming, he asked him to explain what had happened when Henderson had arrived at his station.

'He was quite agitated, sir, understandably,' replied the young constable. 'He told me that he had been in Perth all day and that when he had reached his house, he had been forced to make his way in through the bedroom window, as the kitchen door was locked. He then found his sister murdered. I asked him if the assailant was still in the house at the time, to which he answered no.' Pausing for a second, he then added, 'There was something a bit queer with his answer to that sir, if you don't mind me saying.'

'What was queer?' asked his superior.

'Well, when I asked him that, sir, he blushed.'

'He blushed?'

'Yes sir, very noticeably – cheeks as red as beetroot. I've no idea why he might have done that, but I did find it odd.'

'Thank you, Alex,' replied the superintendent. Turning to Constable Rowley, he then asked for a description of Crichton's demeanour when the labourer had approached him at Forgandenny station.

'He was very calm, sir. He told me there had been a murder at the farm and that I should come at once. Told me that his master had killed his sister, or at least that he believed that to be the case.'

McDonald was somewhat surprised at this. 'He actually accused him of the deed?'

'Yes sir, though when I asked him to say how he could possibly know that, he just said that it must have been him. Reckons he had had plenty of time to do so after his return from Perth. They do have a bit of a history though sir,' added the constable, 'they are none too fond of each other.'

The superintendent thanked them and then dismissed his officers from the kitchen, instructing them to take up positions outside the farm to guard the main entrances.

Satisfied that the site was now secured, the deputy fiscal announced that he would return to Perth to contact the sheriff in order to obtain a warrant for a post-mortem examination to be performed on the victim later that morning. Putting his hat and coat back on, John Young stepped out of the house and awoke the driver of the carriage, who was napping inside the vehicle, and instructed him to return at once back to the city. With a crack of the whip, the conveyance hastily departed.

Reaching the fiscal's office at Perth's County Buildings, Young wasted no time in telegraphing his superior, John McLean, to update him with the situation. Within half an hour, the deputy fiscal had received instructions to arrange for the required warrant from the sheriff's office, and to enlist the help of another physician in the town, Dr George Webster Absolon. McLean had also informed his deputy that he would be on his way south shortly and would arrive at Mount Stewart just after dawn. Young then instructed a constable to summon both the sheriff substitute of the county, Mr Hugh Barclay, and Chief Constable Gordon.

George Gordon was a long-term career officer, a no-nonsense sort who had cut his policing teeth in the County of Edinburgh police force. Originally from Badenoch in Invernesshire, the forty-six-year-old Highlander had for the last decade been in charge of the Perthshire constabulary, and was responsible now for a force which included his superintendent, two inspectors, two detectives, eight sergeants and forty-one constables. In addition to his policing duties for Perthshire, Gordon was also chief constable of the county police forces in Kinross and Clackmannanshire, a procurator fiscal to the justices of the peace, and an inspector for weights and measures. As if his hands were not tied up enough, he had further responsibility for over forty water-bailiffs on the River Tay, with particular care for the salmon fishing industry on the river and its main tributaries.

Following his initial appointment, Gordon had taken a great deal of time to develop the work ethic of his constables, weeding out those incapable of remaining sober and unwilling to fully commit to the observance of the law. At the same time he had also strived to provide better terms and conditions for his men, including his greatest success to date, the construction of new purpose-built police stations for the more rural beats. Gordon had convinced the Commissioners of Supply, the body which oversaw and paid for his force, that such buildings were necessary to provide better residential conditions for his officers, as well as desperately needed secure lock-ups for offenders.

On the accommodation front, the situation in Perth itself was unfortunately much less satisfactory. The offices of the County Constabulary's headquarters were based in a cramped tenement building adjacent to the City Police Force's headquarters on the corner of High Street and the Watergate. The two constabularies were entirely separate, with each jealously guarding their respective jurisdictions, although both maintained a professional working relationship. The City Police Force building contained cells which the County Constabulary rented when it needed to detain a suspect for further questioning after an arrest.

Gordon had formed a good working relationship with Hugh Barclay, the county's sheriff substitute, over the eleven years that they had known each other. Both gentlemen shared the same ideals and philosophy behind the organisation of the constabulary. As the sheriff substitute, Barclay worked under the county sheriff, Edward Strathearn Gordon, though had a much more day-to-day role in dealing with cases at the Sheriff Court, where he presided with the full authority of a judge. He had worked in Perth for some twenty-five years, and in 1851 had written a work entitled *A Digest of the Law of Scotland*, essentially a dictionary on the finer points of Scots Law. Sheriff Barclay had helped to shape the eighty-three regulations to which Gordon's constabulary currently adhered, and these had been reproduced in later editions of his publication as an example to other forces. The first of the regulations had stated the fundamental principal objectives of the force to be 'the prevention of vagrancy and crime'; the remainder had then fleshed out the exact duties and responsibilities of the constables in the fulfillment of their obligations as officers of the law.

As chief constable, Gordon had the power to appoint and dismiss members of the force, as well as to promote and demote individuals whenever he deemed it 'proper for the public service'. His constables were to be at all times civil to the public in the administration of their duty, to be politically and religiously impartial, and to be equally respectful and obedient to their superiors. Each was also to be literate; their career path was dependant on it. 'No constable can be promoted to the rank of serjeant [*sic*] who cannot write a good hand, and make out a correct report, no matter how exemplary his conduct may be,' stated regulation twenty-three. For this reason, it was added, it was in the interest of every constable to devote all free time to reading and writing and 'the general improvement of his mind'.

In recent months Gordon's workload had increased substantially. The new Trespass Act had seen many travellers and tramps forced to settle in some of the more rural villages; they had immediately fallen foul of their neighbours, leading to an increase in the number of disturbances and altercations between them, which in turn constantly required the attendance of his officers. Poaching had also been on the increase in the county, but in the last week two of Gordon's constables had managed a symbolic victory on that front. They had successfully ambushed and arrested a group of four poachers who had been chasing game, aided by a mob, on the Dupplin estate, not far from the Bridge of Earn. Three of the gang, brothers by the name of Murray, had been subsequently jailed by Sheriff Barclay.

Two major developments within the last six months had dramatically added to the chief constable's woes. The first had been the cattle plague. With such a small force to cover a county as large as Perthshire, the policing of animal movement orders had created a huge burden. In the previous week alone five new cases of rinderpest had been reported across the county, and there was no let-up in sight. To make life more difficult, several justices of the peace and other county officials had attempted to direct the chief constable's officers in the more rural areas without his express authorisation through the correct chain of command, leading to many heated written dispatches from the County Constabulary headquarters.

The second event had been the investigation of another murder, which had required the combined efforts of both the Clackmannanshire and Perthshire constabularies to investigate. On Monday, 18 December 1865, the driver of a bread cart, Alexander McEwan, had been found mortally wounded at Vicker's Bridge, a quiet section of road between Dollar and Blairingone. Still alive when found, the carter had been able to tell them that he had been shot and then robbed by a man who had been lurking in a ditch to the side of the track. He had died shortly after. Acting on a tip-off, Joseph Bell had been apprehended just a couple of days later. An English potter by trade from Derbyshire, Bell was known to have been frequenting the area for the last few years as a poacher. When arrested he had defiantly declared that he was not guilty, before being taken to Alloa Jail for detention until a trial could be arranged in a few weeks time. Bell's day in court would be soon; if found guilty, his reward would be an appointment with the hangman.

Now an equally atrocious murder appeared to have been committed. Seated in the constabulary headquarters, both Gordon and Barclay were quickly brought up to date on the proceedings of the evening. At the completion of the briefing, the sheriff departed to get the necessary warrant drafted, promising to have it at the farm within a few hours. Gordon had then arranged for a couple of additional constables to join him and the deputy fiscal. With the arrival of Dr Absolon, the chief constable's party set off for Mount Stewart Farm, arriving at the steading just before the break of dawn on the Saturday morning.

Inside the building, Gordon examined the crime scene and listened intently to a summary of initial findings from his superintendent and sergeant, as well as from Dr Laing. The chief constable asked McDonald for his initial impressions of the three men seated within the adjacent room. The superintendent observed that Crichton seemed very calm, and stated that if he had committed the deed, he would perhaps have been more agitated. Laing agreed. To the doctor's eyes, the ploughman seemed unusually quiet, perhaps almost disinterested in the proceedings, considering the shocking brutality of what had befallen his master's sister. Sergeant Ross concurred, but added that whilst William Henderson was in obvious shock, Barlas was clearly an incidental player to the drama which had unfolded.

There must have been a motive for the killing, observed Gordon. If the killer was sitting in the parlour at present, what possible reason could he have had to carry out such an atrocious act? The kitchen appeared to have been ransacked, but was that as a consequence of an attempt at plunder, or an effort by the culprit to misdirect an investigation? At first light, he determined, a thorough examination of the house would be carried out to see if anything was missing.

———

Dawn broke at a quarter to seven. Having determined that Barlas had only had a minor role to play in the previous evening's events the mason had been duly released, and had returned to his cottage to his anxious wife. Crichton and Henderson were both questioned to confirm the basic chronology of the proceedings of the previous night. With daylight now beginning to slowly illuminate the interior of the house, both gentlemen were ordered to strip off their clothing to the waist in order that Dr Laing could make a complete forensic examination of their garments.

The contrast in the appearance between the two men's clothing was found to be remarkable. Henderson's undergarments had clearly not been changed for a couple of weeks, and showed no sign of any blood. Crichton's attire was equally untouched by blood, but appeared to be spotlessly clean, as if newly put on. Each item was examined in detail for traces of blood, but with no such incriminating evidence discovered, both gentlemen were allowed to redress.

A search was then authorised to determine what damage might have been caused elsewhere in the house. Leaving the hallway, Gordon and his men made their way into Henderson's ground-floor bedroom, with the farmer accompanying them. The room had clearly been ransacked. A large oak trunk used by Henderson to hold his clothes had been forced open; deep gouges were clearly visible in the wood, made by whichever device had been used to prise the lid up from the lock. Searching for the possible instrument, Gordon discovered a pair of broken scissors lying on a dressing table with one of its blades missing. A comparison with the marks on the chest confirmed it to have been the implement used.

A small, grubby pocket book was found by McDonald lying on top of the trunk. Henderson claimed this was normally kept inside but that he had found it earlier on the floor beneath the box. The box itself was empty, but the farmer stated that a sum of money inside had been taken, a few copper coins which he had been keeping for Crichton's son as payment for his assistance at the thrashing of harvested crops. A £1 note was also missing.

A chest in the bedroom was also discovered to have been forced open, again apparently with the use of the scissors, but a silver watch kept within the top drawer had curiously not been removed. An attempt to break into a lockable drawer further down the chest was further found, with the broken point of one of the scissor blades found firmly wedged beside the lock. The bottom drawer had been pulled out completely and lay on the floor in front of it – the clothing within had clearly been rifled through, but no garments appeared to be missing. Henderson noted that the only thing absent was a basket containing a dozen eggs within the press. Eggshells had earlier been found in the kitchen with a half-eaten egg lodged in the ashes of the fire; further fragments of shell were now also found in the bedroom.

The farmer was questioned about the use of a small key found on a bedside table. He revealed that it was for the lock of a chiffonier which sat in a large room on the upstairs floor; it should still have been in the lock, as there was never a need to remove it. The small cabinet was examined but nothing appeared to have been taken.

A little before nine o'clock in the morning, the procurator fiscal, John McLean, arrived at the farm with Sheriff Barclay, who had finally brought the necessary warrant for the two doctors to begin their examination of the deceased. Also accompanying the gentlemen was an architect from Perth called David Smart, who had been brought along to draw up plans of the house; and Constable John Cameron, the second of the force's two criminal investigation officers.

The warrant now available, the main kitchen table and a smaller side table were cleared by Constables Cumming and Rowley and placed together close by the window, the brightest area of the room. The body of Janet Rogers was then lifted with some difficulty from her position on the floor and onto their combined surfaces, with her head placed at the end of the table by the window. Every person in the room was ordered by Gordon to leave, with the exception of the two doctors, the fiscal, Cameron and the chief constable. The post-mortem could now begin.

The two physicians began their examination by first removing the victim's clothes. As a relatively elderly woman at fifty-five years of age, Janet had been quite heavily dressed, making the process of removing her clothing a lengthy procedure. The deceased woman had worn two woollen caps on her head to protect her from the cold, which were now blood-soaked. These were removed first, followed by two tartan shawls and a wincey polka, a short outer jacket which stretched down to her thighs. The doctors then removed her body-length gown and apron. As her dress was removed, Laing discovered a small round snuff box made of tin lodged between her breasts, and handed the item to the criminal officer. Four petticoats of varying materials were then taken off, followed by a pair of stays and two shifts of cotton and flannel. The last items removed were two pairs of stockings. After each item was carefully handed to him, Cameron affixed labels with a relevant description.

By the light of the kitchen window, Laing then assessed the wounds. Dipping a white cloth into a bowl of water, the doctor began by washing away some of the dried blood from her bruised features. He found a skin discolouration known as *ecchymosis* around the left eye and temple, suggesting that a blood vessel had ruptured internally, causing bleeding into the tissues surrounding her eye. Turning her head slightly towards the left, he then examined the wound to the right of the woman's skull. There was an irregularly shaped cut at the bottom of her ear, splitting the cartilage of the lobe, which connected to a deeper wound located directly behind the ear, an inch in length and heavily contused. After gently cleaning this he took a small metal probe and inserted it into the incision, soon establishing that the blow which had caused it had penetrated deep into the woman's large and irregularly shaped temporal bone.

The doctor then tried to examine the top of the woman's head, but found it difficult through her hair, now thick and matted with coagulated blood. Lifting a large pair of scissors from his bag, Laing began to cut off much of the hair, taking several minutes to complete the task. He then washed the top of her head down, to reveal several more wounds to the top of the scalp than had at first been anticipated. There was a very large cut in the centre, about five inches in length; to the left of this were two more running in parallel, one about three inches in length, the other an inch. Additional cuts were also found to the other side of the head. It was obvious that the woman had been struck repeatedly.

Addressing the police officers and the fiscal, Laing then issued a warning of what was to come.

'Gentlemen, although we can observe a series of wounds to the head, we still need to examine the victim's brain and internal organs to fully establish how the death occurred. If either of you have any qualms about this I suggest you leave the room before we commence.' Momentarily hesitating, he then added, 'This will not be pleasant.'

'Thank you Doctor, but we will remain,' replied Gordon, without consulting his criminal officer standing beside him, whose ashen face and fixed gaze betrayed his real feelings on the matter.

For the next hour, the two doctors methodically dissected the corpse before them. Doctor Laing removed the victim's scalp from the skull, a fairly easy process in that it was already loosened to a considerable degree due to the repeated impact of the blows that she had received. Laing lifted the brain and noticed that a small tumour, about the size of a hazelnut, was embedded in the dura mater, one of the main membrane layers covering its exterior. Carefully examining the organ itself, he observed that the shattered temporal bone on the right side of her face had in fact penetrated deep into the brain tissue. The rest of the woman's organs were examined and all found to have been perfectly healthy, though the doctors discovered that her gall bladder contained some twenty-eight gallstones, ranging in size from a barley pickle to a child's marble. A cursory examination of the digestive tract revealed that the victim had eaten not long before the attack, with digestion appearing to have not yet commenced.

The post-mortem completed, the two doctors conferred for a few moments over their findings, before Laing addressed the chief constable and the procurator fiscal.

'The wounds were quite unquestionably the cause of death, with the impacts on the skull having driven fragments of bone into the brain tissue.'

'Can you estimate a time of death, Doctor?' asked McLean.

'We believe that death could not have happened any later than six o'clock in the evening. In fact, it was almost certainly much earlier than that – we suspect that the killing most likely happened in the middle of the afternoon, between two and three o'clock.'

The implications were immediately clear. In many murder cases it was often the person who discovered the victim's body who would later turn out to be the killer. Yet if William Henderson's account of the day was confirmed, it could not possibly have been him. Stepping out of the door, Gordon approached his superintendent.

'Henry, what time did Henderson say that he returned here?' he asked.

'After seven o'clock, sir. And we have had that corroborated by both of the other prisoners.'

'The autopsy has confirmed that Henderson could not have committed this attack. I want you to get every spare man to begin a search of the immediate vicinity for any sign of parties who may have been strangers. Somebody must have seen something untoward in the last couple of days.'

'Yes sir,' replied McDonald.

'Our murderer is still on the loose, Henry. We must find him quickly before he absconds from the area.'

THREE

INVESTIGATION

Throughout the Saturday morning, Gordon's officers performed a sweep of the local countryside around Mount Stewart, searching for any sign of the killer. Constable Cumming made house-to-house enquiries to the north of the farm along the main road to the Bridge of Earn; Constable Rowley did likewise in the nearby village of Forgandenny. Additional officers newly arrived from Perth were dispatched to the surrounding districts of Kintillo, Aberdalgie and Dunning. Locals were asked for any indication of a suspicious character in the neighbourhood, whilst barns and outbuildings were searched.

At the farm, Superintendent McDonald and Constable Cameron made an inventory of all items likely to be considered useful as evidence. They lifted the bedding materials that had been thrown onto the floor and carefully labelled each individual item – a carpet bedcover, a double blanket, two single blankets, two linen sheets, a bolster and its slip. Further exhibits removed included the pair of blood-covered leather boots, a broken pair of tongs found by the fire and various eggshells. Three paper bags which had earlier been discovered on the kitchen table were also marked up, having clearly been handled by the killer after the murder had been carried out. The first, saturated with blood, had the words 'From Stanley Provision Company' printed upon it. Inside were about two ounces of snuff, evidently purchased by Janet from the store near to her home at Airntully. The second was a long, thin package, empty of content but with the words 'From John Taylors' printed on the outside; it too seemed to have contained snuff at some point. The third bag, plain in appearance and also apparently handled by the killer, had been found lying within an upside down basket lid found on the floor. The murder weapon itself – the kitchen axe – was also carefully labelled and removed.

The pipe fragments discovered by McDonald under the bolster on the floor were found to be incomplete. Sergeant Ross had made an extensive search of the kitchen to try to locate the missing pieces, and also within Henderson's bedroom, but they could not be found. The farmer had been asked whether he smoked, to which he had replied that he did not. He further stated that he did not believe that his sister did either, and was surprised at the suggestion that she may have taken snuff.

Working around everybody in the room was David Smart, the architect brought to the farm from Perth by the procurator fiscal. Occasionally interrupting the activities of policemen and witnesses alike, he spent the morning measuring the various dimensions of each of the rooms in order to produce detailed plans of the ground and upper floors. Great attention was given to the kitchen in particular, where he sketched out a plan of the murder scene, recording every chair, window and dresser. The positions of the bedding and clothes were shown covering Janet's corpse, and even the position of the axe, rested against the wall between the box bed and the fire.

Finishing his work inside the kitchen, the architect stepped out into the yard to record a plan for the exterior of the building and its many outhouses. To check Henderson's claim that entry had been physically possible through the small upstairs window, Smart repeated the exercise with the assistance of Constable George Mearns, one of the officers based at constabulary headquarters. Mearns held the rickety ladder in place as the architect climbed slowly up, before disappearing into the bedroom. Returning outside a few minutes later the architect then completed his work by estimating the dimensions of the farm's stables and byre, as well as noting the direction of the paths around the property and towards Crichton's cottage.

The kitchen door remained locked, with the key still not found. Constable Mearns was instructed to search for the missing item in the immediate vicinity of the building. After an initial visual inspection of the yard revealed nothing, he lifted an old spade lying on the ground in front of the barn, in order to clear out a small cesspool located a few feet away from the rear door, close to the track to the west side of the house. Used as a temporary rubbish tip for refuse and dirty water from the kitchen, the small sink-hole was about ten inches wide by eleven inches long at the top, and a foot and a half deep. Over the course of several minutes the officer carefully removed the top few inches of its contents, much of it a filthy mud, and found the bottom after probing through the remaining contents with the spade. He was soon convinced that the key was not there, and after returning the shovel to the large wooden structure where he had found it, continued his search along the track leading down towards the Linnlea cottages.

At midday, a cart pulled up in the yard, carrying two ashen-faced gentlemen in their early fifties and a younger woman in her early twenties, who had evidently been crying for much of the journey. The newly arrived party was greeted by the superintendent, who enquired as to their business.

'My name is James Rogers,' was the stern reply. 'Janet was my wife.' McDonald apologised and after helping the young lady to disembark from the back of the cart, led them both into the house to be introduced to the chief constable.

The news of his wife's sudden death had been relayed to the fifty-seven-year-old labourer earlier that morning whilst he had been working in the woods of the Rohallion estate, near the village of Murthly to the north of Perth. His wife's brother-in-law, Peter Anderson, had ridden out on horseback to find him, imploring the labourer to leave with him at once. Rogers had initially refused, demanding to know what was so important that he had to depart so suddenly. Unable to convince him to come, Peter had told him to prepare himself for the worst, and had then conveyed to him the news that his wife had been brutally murdered. The numbed Rogers had immediately agreed to accompany his kinsman back to his house at Ardoch, near Blackford. With Anderson's eldest daughter Mary, the two men had then travelled out to Forgandenny.

From the parlour, Henderson recognised the sound of his brother-in-law's voice, and stepped out into the hall. Mary threw her arms around her uncle, and began to sob as the pair stood together. The farmer then caught sight of Rogers' blank expression, and lifting his niece's arms from him, stepped towards the labourer.

'I'm sorry James. She was dead when I found her,' he said, solemnly and apologetically.

'Bill, where's Janet?' he replied. 'Where's my wife?'

Turning to the superintendent, Henderson asked whether it was possible to step through to the kitchen. McDonald agreed, but advised that it might be best if the young woman remained in the hall.

With that, the farmer led Rogers down the hallway and into the kitchen, where much of the scene was still as it had been found originally. By the window, Janet's body was still stretched across the two tables, though the wounds made by the post-mortem examination had been stitched up and the body now wrapped tightly in a linen sheet. Rogers walked over towards his wife, and after pausing momentarily, pulled the linen back slowly to reveal her expressionless face. The sight of the wound to Janet's temple startled him, but he soon regained his composure. Leaning forward, he kissed his wife lightly on the forehead, before lifting the sheet back gently over her face. Stepping back, the labourer was shocked to notice that there was a pool of blood beneath where she lay, and that some of the liquid was still on the walls.

'Dear me,' he remarked, 'this room looks like a slaughterhouse.'

Rogers asked the farmer to explain what had happened, and then listened intently to his account of the previous night. Once the farmer had finished, the Airntully man suggested that he would like to get the place cleaned up. Janet should not be leaving the house as if it was her murder scene, he asserted, she should leave the farm in the manner in which she had arrived – with a degree of dignity.

With the permission of the police, the two men set about their work. Fetching pails of water from the well, both returned to the kitchen to begin the task of returning the room to some form of normality, gratefully accepting Peter Anderson's offer to help also. The three men toiled silently, trying not to allow the horror of the task to get in the way of what needed to be done.

———•——

At half past one in the afternoon, the senior officers of the constabulary and the procurator fiscal thanked the physicians for their help in the yard. As the two doctors clambered onto Dr Laing's carriage and set off down the track, Superintendent McDonald turned to Gordon and said, 'It's the Kellocher case all over again, sir.' The chief constable understood the reference. 'Let us make sure this one has as equally successful an outcome, Henry,' he replied, before stepping back into the farm building with the fiscal. Noticing Constable Mearns' confused expression beside him, the superintendent offered an explanation.

'There was a case something quite like this a few years back, lad, very similar in fact. It was a murder just outside of Blackford. The victim was killed with an axe also.' Stifling a yawn, the tired officer continued. 'The villain responsible was caught some months later, and hanged. We have not had an execution in the town since then. It was a terrible business.'

The Blackford killing had happened early in the superintendent's career, McDonald explained. The Perthshire Constabulary had had no formal involvement with the investigation, which had instead been handled by the procurator fiscal's office in Dunblane. On Sunday, 19 November 1848, a young woman by the name of Janet Anderson had been found mortally wounded by her neighbour's children within her house. The victim had been lying senseless on the floor, with a small pool of blood surrounding her head; her injuries so profuse that the woman's brains had been visible to the eye.

Remarkably, this Janet had remained alive for another six hours, but had lost her fight for life later that night at eleven o'clock. A post-mortem examination by two doctors at the scene had confirmed that she had been murdered with a small kitchen axe, which had been found lying beside her on the stone floor. Janet Anderson's house had also been a shop, and with a substantial amount of money discovered to have been removed, the motive had easily been established as robbery.

A strenuous investigation had eventually led to the apprehension of the killer. A navvy by the name of John Kellocher had lodged at the woman's house a few months earlier, whilst working on the construction of a track for the Scottish Central Railway. After two months, the short-term project had finished, and Kellocher had returned to his native Ireland to try and find work as a fisherman with his nephew, John Eagan. The fishing turned out to be poor, and the two men had quickly become desperate to earn some money before their limited funds ran out. After several weeks in Ulster, both men had once again boarded a steamer at Belfast for Glasgow.

Whilst walking on the road to Stirling a few days later, Kellocher had suddenly suggested to Eagan that he was going to murder his former landlady, knowing that she had a substantial amount of money within her house. Despite his nephew's strenuous objections, Kellocher had gone ahead with his dastardly plan. The greatest tragedy of all lay with the fact that Janet had in fact invited him into the house, having been delighted to see him again. An innocent welcome to an old friend had cost the woman her life.

Six months later, the Irishman had been brought to a gallows outside the south end of Perth Jail, a court having found him responsible for the crime despite his passionate plea of not guilty. On the night before his execution, however, he had finally confessed freely to having committed the murder, satisfying the authorities that justice was indeed truly about to be done. At ten minutes past eight o'clock on the following morning, John Kellocher had breathed his last.

As McDonald finished explaining the case history, he was alerted to the sound of running in the yard, as Constable Cumming made his way hurriedly towards him.

'Excuse me, sir,' panted the constable, somewhat out of breath, 'but I think we may have something. I have been talking to some of the residents along the road below. A couple of them claim to have seen a hawker making a turn off for the road towards the farm here yesterday.'

'Do you have a name?' enquired his superior.

'Yes sir. It's Betsy Riley. She lives in Perth, sir. Irish woman, comes out this way quite regularly. Mrs Barlas, the mason's wife, mentioned that she saw her about half past eleven, as she asked her if she wanted anything. The Williamson woman at the shop down the road also mentioned seeing her.'

'Excellent work,' noted McDonald, before instructing Cumming to fetch the chief constable and the fiscal. Turning to Mearns he added, 'Get the carriage ready, George. Let us hope that this Mrs Riley has seen something worthwhile on her travels.'

FOUR

BETSY RILEY

Betsy Riley lived in a small, first-floor dwelling house on Perth's South Street, accessible only by a curved set of worn stone steps from a filthy back court. By five o'clock in the evening she had been located at her home by Constable Cameron and escorted to the procurator fiscal's office, which was located further along the same street.

Aged forty-eight, Riley was the daughter of an Irish weaver, currently working every day as a hawker of earthenware in place of her husband John McKechney, who had been invalided by a stroke a few months earlier. Panicking at Cameron's arrival, she had insisted that she was fully licensed under the Hawkers Act, a breach of which could lead to a fine of £10 by the local magistrate. The constable had calmed her down and assured her that his only interest with Betsy lay with what she might have seen on the previous day at Mount Stewart Farm. He explained that there had been a terrible murder there, and that her testimony was therefore of interest to the investigation now underway. The woman was then told to await the arrival of Mr McLean, who would be conducting the interview.

Minutes later Sheriff Barclay, John McLean and Superintendent McDonald entered the room. The fiscal took a seat directly across the table from the hawker, while the other gentlemen stood to the side. McLean looked directly at Riley and thanked her for attending, before briefly outlining the reasons for her required presence. The context established, he asked her to first explain why she had been in the area of Mount Stewart Farm on the previous day.

Riley nervously pulled her shawl around herself, before answering that she had been out selling dishes in the area between Perth and Glenearn. She explained that as the parochial board was only allowing her a shilling a week to look after her ailing husband, she had been forced to bring in some additional income.

'What time did you set off from Perth?' asked McLean.

'Well I left Perth about nine in the morning, sir, with a basket of dishes, and made my way along the Edinburgh Road. When I reached the Brig I stopped for a bit beside the road to have a smoke. I waited quite a while, and then set off again over the railway crossing. Shortly after this I saw Mr Henderson.'

'The farmer?' interjected the fiscal.

'Yes sir,' replied Riley. 'He was on his cart heading into the village. I guessed he was making for the market in Perth. We never spoke to each other. I'm not even sure the beggar noticed me, to be honest.'

Continuing her testimony, the hawker explained that she had stopped off at the wright's house just before Pitkeathly Wells, but the mistress there had not required anything. Moving on she had next tried the shoemaker further along the road, but again nothing was required from her. At this point Riley had then turned onto the road leading up towards Mount Stewart. She had first called in at the ploughman's house at Linnlea, but had found nobody there, and so had proceeded to the Barlas's house next door. One of the children working in the garden had led her inside, where she had discovered the ploughman's wife talking to Mrs Barlas. Although Mrs Crichton had stated that she required nothing, Mrs Barlas had told her to wait as she fetched some rags for her. In return she had given the mason's wife a small bowl. When the fiscal asked her at which time this had occurred, Riley replied that Mrs Barlas was about to leave her house to get the train to Perth; she surmised that it must therefore have been well after eleven o'clock, with the train due to leave Bridge of Earn at midday. The hawker then explained that after her stop at Linnlea she had walked up the hill towards Mount Stewart Farm.

'Were you hoping to try the farmer next?' asked McLean.

'Oh no, sir, not at all,' replied Riley in her thick Irish brogue. 'I was walking that way to get to the footpath on the other side of Mr Henderson's yard, which leads to Dumbuils Farm. I was not expecting anyone to be in at the farm.' The woman then paused, as if uncertain that she should say what she was about to say. 'There is a lot of talk about, you see sir, about that one and his servants. I heard that he was without one again.'

The fiscal and the superintendent briefly exchanged a glance. 'What sort of talk Mrs Riley?' enquired McLean.

'Well, he's had a few servants in the last few months, sir, they never last more than a week or two. I've heard it said that Mr Henderson tries to offer them more than just a wage.'

Sheriff Barclay interrupted the woman. 'You should watch your tongue with such nonsense Betsy. That could very well be considered as slanderous. Mr Henderson is highly regarded in the area.'

Riley sat up with a mixture of both angry indignation and alarm at the sudden rebuke. 'I'm sorry sir, but that is what they are all saying. I'm only repeating that which I have heard.'

Changing tack, McLean brought her back to the subject at hand, asking her to detail exactly what she had observed as she had approached the farm. Riley explained that as she had stepped into the farmyard she had noticed a woman standing by the kitchen door, whom she now presumed to have been Mrs Rogers. The woman had been holding a small shovel in her hand, which the hawker assumed she had been using to take out some ashes from the fire. When asked to give a description of what she was wearing, Riley replied that she had on a dark grey jacket or polka, and a coarse linen apron. She did not appear to be wearing a dress, but was wearing a dark petticoat, and possibly a black cap on her head.

'Did you speak to her, Mrs Riley?' asked the fiscal.

'I asked her if she had any rags,' replied the hawker, 'but she just replied "no woman", so I left her to continue on with her conversation and walked on.'

At this comment, the fiscal raised his eyebrows. 'Her conversation? Mrs Riley, to whom was she conversing?' he asked.

'Oh I'm sorry, sir. She was talking to a man at the door. I didn't get much of a chance to look at him as he was facing her, but I did manage to get a quick sight of the side of his face when I passed. Sure wasn't there a dog there also, lying on its belly without a care in the world – though that might just as well have been the farmer's as it might have been yer man's.'

When asked if she knew what Janet Rogers and the gentleman were discussing, Riley replied that she had not listened in, but that the tone of the conversation had not seemed in any way to be hostile. McLean then addressed her slowly. 'It is very important, Mrs Riley, that you try to remember exactly how this fellow was dressed, and any other details of his appearance which you might recall.'

Sensing that all eyes were now fixed firmly upon her, Riley provided a lengthy description. She noted that he was about five foot eight or nine inches tall, had a dark shooting coat on, dirty moleskin trousers, and dark cloth cap, which was either black or a dark blue in colour. She could not recall what shoes he was wearing. When asked to describe his face, she replied that she had only briefly managed to get a look at him. He had worn a cap with a long leather peak on the front which had covered his eyes, but, she continued, she did note that he had a swarthy complexion to his skin, and was not clean shaven. She estimated that his age must have been about forty years old; he was neither an old man, nor a youngster.

'Would you say that he was in the same line of work as yourself, Betsy?' asked Superintendent McDonald.

'Oh no sir, his clothes were quite smart, if not perhaps a little dirty. I would not describe him as either a working man or a vagrant.' Riley then focussed her gaze firmly back towards McLean. 'Could he have been the killer, sir?'

'Possibly Mrs Riley, it is too early to tell, but all of this information is certainly very useful,' he offered, reassuringly. 'How long would you say that you were at Mount Stewart?'

'Oh, not long at all, Mr McLean sir. Once Mrs Rogers told me that she required nothing I just carried on to the Dumbuils path, and made my way to Mrs Ritchie's house, which I reached about midday. After chatting to her I then visited Mrs McKerchar, the grieve's wife, at Dumbuils, and from there I made my way to Glenearn and hawked all the houses there.'

'Did you return to Mount Stewart again later?' the fiscal asked.

'No sir, I did not. There is a road that leads directly from Glenearn to the Brig, so I made my way back to Perth on that.'

McLean stood up from the desk and thanked the hawker for her assistance, and suggested that she may need to be spoken to again in due course. He then directed Constable Cameron to escort the woman to the door of the office.

Sensing an opportunity, Riley turned to the sheriff substitute standing at the back of the room. 'Will there be a reward offered sir, if you don't mind my asking? I mean, if this is the killer?'

'It is too early to say Mrs Riley,' replied Barclay, 'though rest assured that you will have our eternal gratitude if this does prove to be of assistance.'

With that Riley turned around and was escorted out of the room by the constable, stubbornly muttering, 'His bloody gratitude is not going to pay my rent,' under her breath as she departed.

No sooner had she left than Sheriff Barclay addressed John McLean and the Superintendent. 'Gentleman, clearly you must have the description of that man circulated immediately.' The Irishwoman had witnessed a possible suspect talking to the victim just hours before her death. Whoever the mysterious stranger was, he had to be located at once.

In the early morning hours of Sunday, 1 April, a low mist crept in silently over the Ochil Hills towards Forgandenny, like a heavy blanket seeking to contain the tragedy lurking within the parish. Word of the murder had spread quickly throughout the area, the vague details of the incident passed by word of mouth from neighbour to neighbour in the surrounding villages. The shocked communities of the lower Strathearn valley had made their way to their respective kirks at Dron, Dunning, Forgandenny and the Bridge of Earn, and listened intently as their ministers asked them to pray for the Henderson and Rogers families at the Sunday morning services.

Throughout the previous night William Henderson and James Rogers had taken it in turns to keep a silent vigil over Janet's body, now wrapped in a sheet but still lying across the two tables in the kitchen. Although Henderson was not considered to be a suspect, the Forgandenny constable, Thomas Rowley, had remained at the farm under orders from his chief constable, along with a colleague from Perth. Both had kept a respectful distance from the grieving men.

Peter Anderson and his daughter Mary had left late on the previous evening to make arrangements with a local undertaker to convey Janet's body back to her family home in Airntully. Despite it being a Sunday, the two men had decided that it was not a day for church, and instead fed and watered the animals, keeping their thoughts to themselves in the early morning cold. The expectant cow in the byre was now more agitated, pacing around inside the structure, which suggested that labour was not too far away.

There was still one important task to be performed within the kitchen. Although the police had taken the clothing in which Janet had been discovered, they had allowed her husband to retain possession of the remaining items within her bedroom on the first floor. Rogers walked upstairs to the room to fetch a dress, and was heartened to find that the item hanging on the bedstead was that which she had always considered to be her favourite. This would be the garment that she would be buried in. In lifting the dress up the labourer was surprised to find that there was a purse and a handkerchief within the pocket, though the purse was quite empty. After removing these he returned to the kitchen.

Understanding what his brother-in-law was about to do, Henderson left the room to allow him some privacy. Rogers gently removed the sheet covering his wife's body, and washed away the remaining blood from her face. With anguished tears silently making their way down both cheeks, he carefully dressed her with the garment in a final moment of duty to his beloved wife.

After his task had been completed, the two men had stepped out of the house, opting to work silently at various jobs around the yard to provide them with a purpose. By mid-morning both had become alerted to the growing noise coming from the byre, which suggested that the cow might be in the latter stages of labour. They hurriedly crossed over to the structure and discovered their suspicions to be correct. The beast was now lying down on its side and lowing painfully. Mucus was emanating from the animal's vulva and the tell-tale sign of a yellow water sac emerging suggested that the animal was about to give birth.

Henderson asked Rogers to fetch a rope hanging on one of the nails on the wall of the building, as he kneeled down at the rear of the animal to assist. He cleared away the mucus and soon the reassuring sight of the calf's hooves began to appear. Mercifully, the bottom of the hooves were pointed downwards, suggesting that the newborn was in the correct birth position. The farmer took a hoof in each hand and began to pull back, gently at first until he was sure that the beast was slowly moving, and then with increased force. Although there was movement, it was minimal. The farmer turned to Rogers and asked for the rope. He tied it around the two hooves and secured it there with a knot, before lifting it up and pulling back hard. Rogers took hold of the rope also and joined in the effort. The young animal's nose soon began to emerge, at which point the whole calf finally slipped out and onto the straw. Henderson checked that the young animal was breathing; thankfully it was. Rogers smiled sadly; amidst the tragedy of death, this newborn life provided a blessed, if temporary, distraction.

Whilst laying down some new straw, Henderson decided to inform his relation about the burglary at the steading a couple of months earlier. The farmer shared his suspicions that Crichton had been responsible for the theft. Rogers listened and agreed with the possibility that the perpetrator of the first crime may well have been that of the second, but cautioned against blaming the ploughman until more evidence could be found. Unable to restrain his despair about the killing any further, Henderson suddenly broke down, the absent tears from the previous two days no longer respecting any barriers, as he openly wept in the byre.

For much of the day the two exhausted men continued to work on the farm. Although the activity about the steading was no different to that of any other Sunday, the place still felt eerily quiet. In the afternoon the factor of the Freeland estate arrived to briefly convey his condolences on behalf of the laird. An hour later he was followed by Constable Cumming, who had come from the Bridge of Earn with instructions from headquarters for the two constables to now leave the premises and to assist with the house-to-house enquiries in the vicinity.

Later that evening Henderson and Rogers returned to the byre to check on the progress of the newborn calf, and found it lying asleep beside its mother. They also fed the horses, before making their way back to the farmhouse in order to have some supper, though neither man was really that hungry. Both men failed to notice that James Crichton was standing behind a tree to the side of the track that led to the front door.

As they entered the building, they heard the sound of an item being dropped in the kitchen at the far end of the hallway. Henderson stepped forward and threw open the door. Inside, he was surprised to find a young woman standing over the box bed, searching through the bedding for something that was clearly eluding her. On hearing the door's squeaking as it opened, she instantly spun around, revealing herself in the candlelight to be in her early twenties, with long auburn hair and in the clothing of an ordinary domestic servant. Terrified at having been discovered, she lifted her skirts and quickly rushed past both Henderson and Rogers, before running hurriedly towards the front door of the house. The startled farmer pursued her to the doorway, but she was gone before he could utter a word. In fury, he slammed the big wooden door shut and threw over a bolt to secure it firmly, before returning to the kitchen, his face reddened at the audacity of what he had just observed.

'Bill, who was that woman?' enquired a confused Rogers.

'I'm sorry, James. That was my former housemaid, Christina Miller. I dismissed her from service over a week ago.'

Although teetotal, the farmer opened the door of one of the presses in the kitchen and lifted out a bottle of whisky, which he kept purely for medicinal reasons. He lifted a glass and poured out a dram, downing it in one. As his nerves calmed, he explained to his brother-in-law that it was because of such impertinence that he had dismissed the woman in the first place.

'What did she want?' asked Rogers.

'I have absolutely no idea,' replied Henderson, pouring himself another dram and one for the labourer. 'But I'll be damned if she ever gets back in again.'

The two men seated themselves down beside the fire, their faces solemn as they sipped from their glasses, just feet away from the corpse of their loved one.

———•———

As dawn broke on the morning of Monday, 2 April, Rogers made his way from the farmhouse to the byre to check again on the newborn calf. The young animal's imminent arrival had been the reason for his wife's journey to Mount Stewart – now that it had been born, the labourer felt a strange connection to it, the promise of its new life somehow acting as a minor comfort for that which had been so tragically lost. The calf was now on its feet and taking milk from its mother, an image of perfect health that simultaneously brought both a smile and a tear to the labourer as he watched.

At the sound of the stable door opening nearby, Rogers turned and saw Crichton leading one of the horses out for his day's work. Henderson had told him on the previous day that he believed the ploughman to have been the killer. Although he had cautioned the farmer to be wary of such claims, he had yet to speak to the man himself. Now would be his only opportunity.

'This murder is an awful business,' said Rogers, as he walked towards the stable.

'Aye, that it is,' acknowledged Crichton, as he led the horse out into the yard by the bridle.

'I am heartened to hear from my brother-in-law that the police think he is innocent. I had heard that many people suspected him.'

'I don't know about that,' said Crichton gruffly, as he worked to connect a harness to the animal. 'There's nothing too bad for the likes of him.'

Rogers ignored the comment, well aware of the friction between master and servant.

'You were here all day Mr Crichton. Did you see anybody talking to my wife?'

'Aye, I saw the woman talking in the morning to a man at the door.'

'At what time was that?'

'About eleven o'clock.'

'Your master was away to Perth an hour before that, Mr Crichton, it has been well established.'

'I suppose he was.'

'Well then, how could he have killed her?' asked Rogers.

'I reckon he had opportunity enough in the evening,' replied Crichton, still not making eye contact with his interrogator.

Rogers continued to press for more information. 'You saw him in the evening before he found her. Where did you leave him when you went home after your work?'

'I left him by the stable. It was some time before he came near my house after. But it was time enough.'

Rogers was now becoming angered at the ploughman's dismissive attitude. 'Your master did not kill my wife Mr Crichton. I've known the man for over thirty years.' He stepped forward so that he and Crichton were face to face.

'So that means her killer had to be someone else. I hope we discover who it is soon, Mr Crichton.'

Clearly not intimidated, the Fife man stepped away and took the now harnessed beast by the bridle. 'I hope you do find him also, Mr Rogers,' he answered, before bidding the labourer good day and leading the horse towards the field to the west of the steading.

———

At midday the sound of a heavy carriage arriving in the yard was heard from within the farmhouse. Henderson stepped out to the yard and directed the undertaker from Perth and his men to bring the coffin into the kitchen through the south-facing door of the property. Once inside, Janet's body was carefully laid into the huge wooden box by her husband and brother, before the top was screwed down. Henderson and Rogers then assisted the undertaker's men in carrying the coffin back out of the house towards the hearse in the yard, ready for her transportation to the family home. As the box was loaded onto the vehicle, the farmer observed Crichton watching discretely from the field, as he continued to plough a straight furrow in their direction.

With the coffin finally secured in the vehicle, Rogers embraced Henderson and then climbed onto the hearse to sit beside the undertaker. The Airntully man could also see the ploughman in the distance, but said nothing to his brother-in-law about their conversation earlier in the day. As the vehicle started to make its way down the track, Janet Rogers departed from Mount Stewart Farm for the very last time, in the same manner as her father had done some thirteen years before.

FIVE

HANDBILLS AND INTERVIEWS

Chief Constable Gordon returned to Mount Stewart Farm on the Monday morning, accompanied by Sheriff Barclay and Procurator Fiscal McLean, to make another full search of the premises for additional clues which might have been missed from the initial examinations. Barclay was shown the farmer's bedroom, and the damaged chests and drawers, while the architect David Smart, also in attendance, completed his sketches. A moment of optimism arose when a key was discovered in an upstairs bedroom. At first believed to be the missing kitchen door key, the farmer confirmed that it was in fact the key of a gig or coach house in the yard, which usually remained in his downstairs bedroom. The exhaustive search revealed nothing further and the party once again departed for Perth by early afternoon.

Despite the ferocity of the attack on Janet Rogers, and the appalling state of the property, there was surprisingly little evidence for the constabulary to act on. It was almost certainly the case that plunder had been the motive, but there were numerous possibilities as to how the events may have unfolded at the scene. Had the victim known the killer and brought him into the kitchen, for example, as Janet Anderson had once done many years before in Blackford? Had the burglar forced his way in and overcome the poor woman before attempting to steal items from the house? Had she perhaps discovered his presence and attempted in some way to challenge him? William Henderson's presence in Perth had been well corroborated, but exactly where had the ploughman Crichton been throughout the day?

For the moment, the description of the man witnessed at the farm by Betsy Riley was their strongest lead. A handbill was printed on the Monday morning, but to prevent an initial panic it avoided any description of a murder, simply stating the description of the wanted man.

NOTICE

If any person can give information as to a Man seen on
SATURDAY last, in the Neighbourhood of BRIDGE of EARN,
answering to the annexed description, or if any Person finds
a Large DOOR KEY in that Neighbourhood, they are requested
immediately to inform the PROCURATOR FISCAL at PERTH.

Fiscal's Office, Perth

2nd April 1866

DESCRIPTION

A Man between 40 and 50 years of age
About 5 feet 9 inches in height
Slender make. Thin in figure
Long face. Brown Hair.

DRESS

Dirty Darkish Dress
Wore a Cap.
Dark Frock-Tailed Coat.
Longish Greyish Coloured Trousers.
Shabby Genteel Appearance
Did not look like a Working Man, neither did
he resemble a Hawker or Vagrant.

PRINTED AT THE PERTHSHIRE JOURNAL OFFICE.

The bill was posted in the villages around the farm, as well as in nearby
Perth, whilst the suspect's description was also communicated to the local
county police stations within the area and further afield. Each constable was
instructed to try to find the suspect's whereabouts, but also to keep an open
mind as to the possible identity of the killer.

Whilst Gordon had tried to withhold the actual detail of the crime committed
from the handbills, a much more effective means of print communication was
about to unleash every salacious detail of the tragedy and the investigation's
progress to date. From the first reports of the murder journalists had scoured

the vicinity around Mount Stewart for as much information as could be found, and had even spoken to some of the local witnesses questioned just hours before by officers from the constabulary. The public was now about to read its first independent accounts of what had happened on the outskirts of Forgandenny village, though some reports would be more accurate than others.

The Edinburgh-based *Scotsman* noted the murder as 'a distressing and mysterious case' but erroneously explained that according to a statement made by a witness in the village, a man and two women, apparently all hawkers, had been seen travelling towards Mount Stewart Farmhouse on the Friday. In its coverage, the *North British Daily Mail* described the event as 'a horrible murder'. It opined as to the motive, noting that it was strange that no robbery seemed to have been involved, despite the obvious fact that the house had been ransacked by the assailant. The paper also included the full text of the farmer's note to the procurator fiscal as dispatched from the train station at the Bridge of Earn, but noted with regret that there was still no direct trace of who the guilty party or parties may have been.

The *Dundee Courier* provided the most detailed coverage, describing the event as 'a most revolting and cold-blooded murder', and noting that it seemed 'destined to gain as melancholy a prominence as the Sandyford atrocity'. The paper was referring to a killing committed in Glasgow some four years earlier, when a servant called Jessie McLachan had been found murdered in the basement of 17 Sandyford Place, her head having been brutally attacked with a cleaver. A former servant of the premises called Jessie McPherson had been found guilty of the atrocity a few months later and was sentenced to death. Following the petition of some 50,000 Glaswegians, incensed at several irregularities in the evidence and the nature of the trial, this was reduced to fifteen years' imprisonment. In its haste to break the Mount Stewart story, the paper mistakenly named the owner of the farm as Robert Henderson, before explaining the circumstances by which he had come to find his sister's body and his subsequent notification of the procurator fiscal.

The story was now well publicised and in the wider public domain. From this moment on the eyes of the nation would follow every twist and turn of the current investigation.

———

On the following morning of Tuesday, 3 April, Gordon remained at his headquarters on Perth's High Street, where he received progress reports from his men across the county and examined the evidence gathered from the farm. At lunchtime he composed a letter to William Dyott Barnaby, the chief clerk at Bow Street Magistrates Court in London, in which he outlined a summary of the details as known so far, in order that they might be inserted into the next edition of *The Police Gazette*. The newspaper, first established in 1772 by John Fielding under the title of *The Weekly Pursuit*, was published each Monday and distributed to all police forces across the British Isles, as well as to magistrates, mayors and other high-ranking dignitaries within law enforcement circles. It was an effective means of alerting other police forces across Scotland as to the situation in Perthshire.

Just after midday, an urgent telegram was received by the County Constabulary's office. The message had been sent by a police constable at the ferry station in Burntisland, in the neighbouring county of Fife, who explained that he had apprehended a gentleman appearing to match the description as given in the handbills. The only possible way to confirm if this was indeed the suspect was to have him brought to Perth in order for him to be confronted by Betsy Riley. Gordon immediately instructed his superintendent to travel to Burntisland on the next available train.

Taking Constable Cameron with him, McDonald pushed his way through the many keen reporters now waiting outside the door of the constabulary headquarters for any further news and climbed onto a waiting gig, directing the driver to take them to the General Railway Station. Having opened some eighteen years previously, Perth's main train station had quickly developed into a noisy, clanking, steam-filled hub of activity, with the Caledonian, North British, Scottish North-Eastern and Highland Railways all competing for trade across the country. The latest in a series of major extension works was currently underway to facilitate the rapid expansion of the network, which had transformed communications across the country in such a short space of time. The superintendent and his criminal officer climbed on board the next North British Railway service that would take them south towards Burntisland. A blow of the whistle signalled the steam train's departure.

It took more than two hours to reach the police station in the small village. McDonald was immediately taken to the prisoner, and was soon satisfied that he did bear some resemblance to the description as given. Questioned as to his whereabouts on the day of the murder, the suspect explained that he was a writer, and had been in Perth on the previous Thursday, where he had called at several offices within the town. Just prior to midday he had then set off for Dundee, but, due to the poor state of the roads, had only made it as far as Longforgan, and had been forced to spend the night at an inn. On the following morning he had continued to Dundee. The writer protested that he had spent the whole day and much of the evening there, and could not possibly have been responsible for whatever the crime was that he was alleged to have committed.

McDonald informed him that he would have to be taken to Perth to have his account verified. With the writer transferred into his custody, the superintendent then asked the local Fife-based constable to telegraph Perth with the news that both he and Cameron were returning with the prisoner.

At 9.30 p.m. the party once more reached Perth, with the suspect then immediately conveyed to the constabulary headquarters on High Street. He was led into a darkened room, barely lit by a small gas light and a couple of candles, and instructed to sit down and wait in the presence of one of the duty constables. Half an hour later, the door opened and Betsy Riley was led inside by McDonald and asked to stand before the writer. Holding a candle up to the prisoner's face the superintendent asked the woman to confirm that this was the person she had seen at the farm on the day of the murder. The hawker took a step closer to the suspect and examined him closely, but with a sudden sniff of contempt she walked over to the superintendent and stated that this was most definitely not the man she had seen. Although asked to take her time to make sure of herself, she responded that she did not need a second further, for this was surely not him. A frustrated McDonald then gave the instruction for Riley to be escorted back to her residence, and for the suspect to be conveyed to a cell in the City Police office. He would spend the night here until the claims of his movements in Dundee were verified, the superintendent informed him, despite his suspicion that his story would almost certainly now turn out to be true.

Before leaving the room, Riley turned to McDonald once more and revealed the surprise news that William Henderson had been to see her at her house in Perth earlier that afternoon. The farmer had asked her to tell him about the suspect that she had seen, but when she had answered with the description that she had already given to the police, he had seemed unwilling to believe her. At one point he had even pressed her to consider whether the description of the man could not have been that of the farm ploughman instead, but she had denied the possibility. Concerned at his aggressive tone she had told him to leave her alone, as the police were now investigating the matter, and at this point he had left angrily. The superintendent thanked her for her time and apologised that she had been so accosted; he stated that it would not happen again, but that the police would still require her co-operation in due course. Satisfied that she had received an apology from someone in authority, the hawker stepped out of the room.

The detained writer was released on the following morning, his alibis in Dundee and Longforgan having easily been confirmed by local enquiries.

Thanks to the press coverage, word of the murder was now spreading like wildfire throughout the burgh and surrounding countryside. The decision was taken on Wednesday, 4 April, to have a new handbill printed, and on this occasion no details were spared.

MURDER

DURING the day time on Friday, the 30th March last, JANET HENDERSON or ROGERS, was barbarously MURDERED in the Kitchen of the FARM HOUSE of MOUNT STEWART, in the Parish of Forgandenny, and County of Perth, by some person or persons at present unknown.

From the appearance of the Body and Furniture, in said House, there is every reason to believe that the party or parties who committed the said Crime, must have been considerably covered with blood.

With the exception of a LARGE OUTER-DOOR KEY, nothing has been missed from said house which can again be identified. About Noon on said day, a man of the following description, supposed to be the Murderer, was seen at the Kitchen door of said house:-

Between 40 and 50 years of age. About 5 feet 9 inches in height. Brown Hair, and Small Dark Whiskers. Long Face. Slender make, and thin in figure. Dressed in a dirty darkish Cap., Dark Frock-tailed Coat, rather long; Grayish coloured Trousers. Rather Seedy appearance. Did not look like a working man. He is supposed to have had a small dog, of a dark or grayish colour, along with him.

It is earnestly requested that any information relative to the matter, may be immediately communicated to the Procurator Fiscal, or Chief Constable of County Police, at Perth, or to any Police Constable.

County Police Office,
PERTH, 4th April, 1866.
C.G. SIDEY, PRINTER, PERTH.

On the same day the Perthshire constabulary was joined by Detective Officer James Leadbetter from the City of Edinburgh police force. The presence of the thirty-year-old officer, a native of the town of Borthwick, had been requested by Sheriff Barclay to cast an independent eye over the progress of the investigation so far. Although Gordon now had two full-time detectives on his staff, the Perthshire force's specialist criminal investigation capability was still very much in its infancy, having only been established a couple of years previously in 1864. With such a major investigation now underway it was felt prudent to make sure that all avenues were being correctly pursued.

The Edinburgh detective was fully briefed on the status of the investigation by Superintendent McDonald. He examined the fragments of the pipe and the tin top which had been found at the scene of the crime, and other items of evidence such as the bags of snuff and the eggshells, though was informed that the plans of the building had yet to be completed by the local architect. The superintendent then informed him that Constable Cameron and the procurator fiscal were shortly to venture out to the farm in order to take statements from both the farmer and his ploughman. He suggested that it would be a good opportunity for him to examine the premises for himself and to meet the inhabitants of the 'toun'. Leadbetter had readily agreed to the proposal.

The fiscal's party arrived at Mount Stewart Farm by early afternoon. In the yard they found James Crichton, who directed them to find his master in the byre. The farmer was sweeping out the wooden building, the cow which had given birth a few days before now gone, having returned to the field with its newborn on the previous day. Henderson was introduced by the fiscal to Leadbetter and then informed that he was to be formally interviewed about his movements on the day of the murder.

The farmer led the fiscal and the three investigators towards the house, but before the interview would commence Leadbetter asked to be shown around the property. As the fiscal took the Edinburgh man into the kitchen, Cameron suggested that he would wait outside the building for a few moments to inform the ploughman that he too would be required for an interview.

The criminal officer had an ulterior motive for wishing to talk to Crichton. He approached the stable, and found him brushing down one of the horses. In front of the labourer the criminal officer lifted out his pipe from his coat pocket and filled it with a small pinch of tobacco, before lighting it with a safety match. Noticing the pipe, Crichton commented on its fine appearance.

'Forgive me, Mr Crichton,' responded the constable. 'How rude of me – would you care for a smoke yourself?' he asked, offering the pipe to the big labourer.

'No thank you, Mr Cameron sir. I am not in the habit,' replied the ploughman.

The policeman conversed politely with the Fife man for a couple of minutes about the magnificent horses that he had to work with. With his smoke finished, he then advised the ploughman that they would need to question him also, and so would meet him within the hour at his cottage. At this point Cameron then returned to the farmhouse.

Inside the kitchen, the questioning of William Henderson commenced with discussion of his return from Perth on the previous Friday night, and the discovery of his sister's body. The farmer confirmed that his ploughman had told him that he had seen his sister talking to a stranger in the yard at about eleven o'clock in the morning – this may have been the same person that Betsy Riley had claimed to see, although it appeared to have happened a good hour before her apparent encounter.

The fiscal turned to the issue of the missing kitchen door key. Henderson described how the front door of the property was generally kept locked, with the key left in the rusty lock on the inside. The farmer and his employees mainly used the kitchen door to gain entry to the house on most days. After entering the building through the upstairs window, Henderson stated that he had unlocked the front door himself in order to fetch help from Barlas. From this he observed that the culprit who had committed the murder must have gone out through the kitchen door and taken the key with him, after locking the door from the outside.

The fiscal then asked the farmer to describe his domestic situation at the farm prior to the murder. Henderson responded that he had been a tenant at Mount Stewart for some twenty-one years, and that he usually resided in the building alone, except for the occasional presence of a female servant. Her role, when he had such an employee, was to look after the cleaning, domestic chores and some other additional farm jobs, such as the feeding of chickens and the milking of the cows.

'You have had many servants in your employment recently, Mr Henderson,' stated McLean. 'Can you explain why that is?'

'Good servants are in short supply,' replied the farmer. 'My previous long-term housekeeper, Jane Thomson, came into the family way at the end of last year and I was forced to let her go. Since then I have been forced to use temporary agency staff from one of the servants' register offices in Perth.'

'Who was your last servant?' enquired Leadbetter.

'Her name was Christina Miller. She was in my employment for just two weeks, before leaving on the Thursday last, the week before the murder.'

The Edinburgh detective then sought to deliberately provoke the farmer. 'From what I am led to believe, Mr Henderson, you have something of a reputation with your staff,' he suggested. 'Was your relationship towards this Miller lass in any way untoward? Is this why she left after such a short period in residence here?'

Henderson angrily denied the allegation. If anything, it had been the opposite, he explained. Having taken the girl on, he had very quickly come to regret the decision. Whilst Miller was an attractive woman, he commented that the hounds of Hell could not make the women shut up. She often 'gabbered' and was forever making inappropriate suggestions. Asked to elaborate on the latter part of his comment, he explained that just a couple of days after her arrival she had suggested that what he really needed in his house was the attention of a wife. He assumed that she was placing herself forward for the position, and had told her to watch her tongue and to get on with her work.

A few days later, he continued, the woman who kept the servants' register in Perth, Mrs Lockersie, had then made a visit to his farm to enquire as to how Miller was performing. She had been given tea by the servant and there had been a great deal of talk in the kitchen. When she had eventually departed, Miller had suggested that he should make her employer the mistress of the house, again claiming that he needed a good wife. At this point she had laughed, and had flirtingly suggested that until he gained one she would do her very best to look after him. He had once more chastised her and told her to mind her own business.

'Did you take advantage of what you perceived to be these advances, Mr Henderson?' pressed the fiscal.

'Dear God, no. I had no interest in the woman,' he replied. 'It wasna' me she became chief with. It was Crichton.'

McLean asked him to explain what he meant by this. Henderson explained how his servant had soon turned her attention towards the ploughman, flirting with him on every occasion that he had passed by the kitchen door. Whether she was trying to make the farmer jealous or was genuinely in pursuit of Crichton's affections, despite his being a married man, he neither knew nor cared to know. The atmosphere continued to sour between them, however, and she had soon barred him from even entering his own kitchen. He recalled how on one occasion she had lifted a pair of tongs from the fire to him whilst the ploughman was within earshot, and had loudly threatened to hit him with them if he so much as took a step over the kitchen door. Henderson had warned her that he would dismiss her if she continued to act so recklessly.

The following day, Miller had suddenly disappeared from the farm. It was not until the next morning, a Thursday, that the farmer had discovered her in the early hours of the morning lying asleep in the byre. Infuriated, he had demanded an explanation. A flustered Miller had informed him that she had travelled into Perth the day before to visit Mrs Lockersie. Spending the day in the town, she had not returned to Mount Stewart until late at night. Finding the kitchen door secured, she had rapped it hard for her master to come out from his room to unlock it, but there had been no answer. Henderson explained to the policemen that he had deliberately not answered the door as he had no idea who it might have been so late in the evening.

The farmer had informed Miller that her behaviour was totally unacceptable, at which point the woman had suddenly become insolent towards him, threatening him with her family, her agency, Crichton, anyone that she could think of. In what had developed into a furious argument between him and his servant, the ploughman had stepped in, threatening to hit his master if he should lay so much as a finger on her.

'He threatened to hit you?' asked a surprised McLean. 'What happened then, Mr Henderson?'

'I informed her that she was now dismissed from my service. I gave instructions to Crichton to lift her chest of belongings from the kitchen and take it down to his house, before I did likewise with him.'

'Why did you feel it necessary to dismiss the woman?' asked the fiscal.

'She was getting too intimate with Crichton, and undermining my authority with the man. I was having none of it. That was the last I saw of the woman before Janet's death.'

The venom in Henderson's voice then diminished, as he suddenly realised the outcome of his fateful decision to seek a replacement. 'It left me with a situation, Mr McLean. One of my cows was about to labour. That is why I fetched Janet down a few days later to help in her place. Thanks to that damned woman's insubordination my sister is now dead.'

The questioning turned to the farmer's relationship with Crichton. Henderson explained that he had been in his employment from Martinmas of the previous year, and was due to stay for six months until Whitsun. If it was not for the fact that he desperately needed his services just now, he would have happily dismissed him for insolence a week ago also. He explained his suspicions that Crichton had stolen money from his house a few months before and that he believed that the ploughman may have been the killer.

'Mere suspicion will not be enough, Mr Henderson,' the fiscal replied. 'I understand how you must feel, but what we need is evidence. There is as yet no proof that Crichton was involved in either the burglary or the murder. Do you have such evidence, Mr Henderson?'

The farmer conceded that he held no proof. There was one thing that he had found odd on the day of the killing, however. On the Friday evening after his return from Perth, he had noticed that Crichton had been wearing a clean set of clothes – they were certainly not the items he had worn earlier in the day.

At this the fiscal glanced at Cameron, who acknowledged that this was a new revelation. McLean leant towards William. 'What was he wearing when you left, Mr Henderson?'

'When I gave him his instructions in the morning he had dark clothes on him. In the evening when the doctors examined us both here, he was wearing a white jacket and shirt, and different trousers. I'm no' suggesting that proves anything, Mr McLean, but why would an innocent man suddenly change his clothes in the middle of a working day?'

'Why indeed?' agreed McLean. 'I will certainly put that to Mr Crichton.'

Outside the cottages at Linnlea the two policemen and the fiscal found the ploughman's children at play in the garden, whilst the labourer was himself gathering some coals from a small stone bunker for the fire. Crichton led the party into the cottage and introduced them to his wife, Martha, who bid them to sit at the table. To their surprise, there was one further guest inside. The ploughman explained that this was Henderson's former servant, Christina Miller.

'Indeed? We have just been hearing so much about you,' said the fiscal to the servant, as her face reddened with embarrassment. 'May I ask why she is here Mr Crichton?'

'She is related to my wife,' answered the labourer. 'When Henderson threw her out, I brought her chest down from the farm for storage. She appeared on Sunday to reclaim it, but she is staying with us for a few days until she can have it picked up.'

The fiscal asked Martha if she and Christina could leave the cottage for a short time to allow her husband to be questioned. She lifted a shawl and stepped out of the cottage with Miller, stating that they would take the children for a walk to Forgandenny village.

With the cottage now vacated, the investigators sat down to question Crichton. The fiscal first asked the labourer whether he had seen Janet Rogers on the day of the murder. Crichton answered that he had witnessed her talking to her brother in the morning before his departure for Perth, though had not known that she was his sister – he had assumed that she was just another servant.

'Did you see Mrs Rogers at the door during the day?' asked McLean.

'No, not after her conversation with her brother,' replied the labourer, his answer appearing to contradict what Henderson claimed to have been told.

'Mr Henderson claims that you told him that you had observed somebody about the yard at around eleven o'clock that day?' suggested the fiscal.

'The man's mistaken,' was the dispassionate reply.

McLean continued. 'Did you notice anybody else about the farm at all during the day?'

'Aye, I did. When I was ploughing the field in the afternoon I did see a man walking down the foot road from Dumbuils, the path which cuts through the farm buildings.'

'At what time was this, Mr Crichton?' asked Leadbetter.

'About three o'clock. The dog was with me, and it started barking, before following him into the field beneath the one where I was working. He was some distance away, so I never got a good look at him.'

'Can you provide any sort of description?' continued the detective.

'He was dressed in dark clothes, maybe middle-aged.'

'And this was definitely in the afternoon?'

'Aye, I had already removed the fence posts and was at the ploughing when it happened.'

McLean redirected the conversation. 'Mr Crichton, what clothes were you wearing on the morning of the murder?'

'I had a white moleskin jacket on, a vest and trousers,' replied Crichton.

'It has been claimed that you were in fact wearing darker clothes that morning,' said the fiscal, 'and that you changed them during the day at some stage.'

'That's not true,' replied the labourer. 'They were clean on the day before, on the Thursday. In the morning I had been ploughing in the field and had gotten my trousers wet and torn. I changed them for my Sunday clothes that afternoon, so that I could attend the kirk at Dron for the Fast Day service. My wife then planned to wash the dirty clothes later that afternoon or on the Friday morning. When I returned from the kirk I changed again into clean work clothes before working in the corn yard that evening.'

McLean offered another scenario. 'You say that you caught a hare that morning, Mr Crichton. Did you perhaps get some blood on your garments from this? Perhaps you changed your clothes during your dinner break?'

The ploughman refused to deviate from his story. 'I did not change my clothes on the Friday, Mr McLean sir. I had the same clothes on me when I was working as I had on when your doctors examined me in the evening.'

McLean then asked the ploughman about his relationship with his master.

'Mr Henderson alleges that you threatened to hit him on the week before last, Mr Crichton – over Miller. Is that correct?'

'The man's a fool,' responded Crichton, the lack of respect for his employer plainly obvious.

'Did you threaten to hit him, Mr Crichton?' the fiscal asked again.

'I'll no' watch any man treat the lass the way he did, Mr McLean. I didna' touch him, sir, but I made damned sure he didna' touch her. We only work for the man – we'll no be abused by him.'

'Henderson claims he dismissed the woman because she was getting too intimate with you, Mr Crichton.'

'I told you – the man's a fool. I'm no' the one around here with the reputation for trying to bed his maids. But I ken what the man says. He says a lot of things. He thinks I broke into his house a few months back and that I stole his money.' The labourer looked the fiscal straight in the eye. 'I'm no' that stupid Mr McLean. And I ken also what he says about the lass and why he released her. She's welcome to stay here until she gets herself another position. And damn the man if he has a problem with it.'

SIX

THE FUNERAL

Having been returned from Mount Stewart Farm on the Monday, Janet Rogers' coffin had since lain in her home at Airntully for the next three nights. The funeral had been arranged for the early afternoon of Thursday, 5 April, with the burial due to take place at the kirkyard of Auchtergaven parish, where many members of the Rogers family had previously been laid to rest. Although Airntully was a small village, comprised of just a few buildings, a constant stream of friends and neighbours had travelled from neighbouring farms and settlements to express their condolences throughout the week. Now on the day of the funeral itself they gathered again in large numbers outside of the house to pay their final respects.

In older times the burial of a loved one was a time shrouded with many customs borne from beliefs in the supernatural. It was the traditional role of women to clean and 'kistan', or place, the body into the coffin, after which it would then be watched prior to the funeral in a 'lyje-wake' or 'waukan'. This was sometimes a merry occasion and at other times sombre, where friends and relatives could convey their regards and touch the body as a mark of respect. After the burial, the excessive hospitality would continue at the 'dirge' or 'dredgy', to the point where some families would become heavily indebted for many months and sometimes years ahead. The 'decent burial' was all that many simple folk could hope for in life, and few families would bear the shame of not providing for such. Although the world had entered a more enlightened age, some of the older customs had survived in the quiet Perthshire village. In the Rogers home the mirror in the bedroom was covered and the clock in the main sitting room stopped, in order that Janet's soul would not be confused or distracted.

Janet's younger sisters, Isobel Anderson and Margaret Anderson, had travelled to the village on the Wednesday from their respective homes in nearby Little Dunkeld. Her eldest daughter, Janet Paton, had also made her way north from Blackford, accompanied by her husband William, to grieve with her family. The victim's aunts and uncles were all long deceased on her mother's side, but several cousins from the neighbouring parish of Madderty had made the journey across country. Her father's elderly siblings, James Henderson and Alexander Henderson from Dundee, had both returned, numbed by the appalling circumstances that had brought them back to their home parish to bury one of their own. The uncle that Janet had hoped to hear from, Dr Henderson, now in his early eighties, had also made the journey from Perth by train to neighbouring Stanley, where he had been met by a nephew and brought to the nearby village.

William Henderson arrived in Airntully shortly after lunchtime, having travelled alone by cart from Forgandenny. Whilst readying himself at Mount Stewart early in the morning, he had made yet another discovery concerning the day of the murder which had further angered him. A vest he had intended to wear was found to no longer fit him properly, prompting him to search the house for his only other vest, it being strangely missing from his bedroom. The item could not be found, and a subsequent examination of his entire wardrobe soon revealed that a cloth cap and a pair of trousers had also disappeared. Having believed that only a small amount of money had been taken by the killer, the farmer had now realised that these items of clothing must also have been removed. He resolved to inform the police as soon as he had returned from the service.

The farmer dismounted from his cart and secured the horse, before making his way through the gathering crowd outside the Rogers house, ignoring the faint but obvious whisperings of many who suspected him to have been in some way involved in the tragic deed. It pained him to note that many of those so whispering were long-term friends of the family; some of them were once children he had grown up with. Stepping inside he was greeted by his brother-in-law and nieces, and immediately made to feel the comforting warmth and strength of family that so often only expresses itself in times of great distress. For an hour the Rogers and the Hendersons remained within to bid their final farewells to Janet amongst many tears and expressions of sorrow, particularly the women, who, as was customary, would not be attending the funeral itself.

After the offering of a short prayer, Janet's coffin was lifted by several of the menfolk and conveyed outside to a waiting hearse. As tears poured down their faces, her daughters held onto one another tightly for support at the sight of their mother's coffin being lifted onto the ornate box carriage for her final journey. An effort had been made to raise funds to hire a decent vehicle for the forthcoming burial, a ceremony which in times past had been a simple affair for the poorer labouring classes of rural society, but one increasingly being influenced by the more expensive and metropolitan Victorian practices of the cities. So highly held was Janet in the eyes of many of her kin, and so revolted was the public by the means of her demise, that the money had been easily secured, with no expense spared for the occasion. A mourning coach followed behind the hearse carrying her distressed husband, her brother and elderly uncles, whilst a long procession of friends and neighbours followed on foot, the journey to the kirk being just over a mile away.

As the cortege made its way to Auchtergaven Kirk, Henderson reflected in silence, as a torrent of emotions coursed its way through him. In passing familiar landmarks he recalled the life he had previously enjoyed with his sister in their youth, and the relationship they had continued to enjoy long after both he and their father had moved south. The memories rapidly disappeared as a heavy burden of guilt overcame him for having asked Janet to come to Mount Stewart the week before. This was accompanied by the further thought that if his niece had made her way to his farm, as he had first asked, it may well have been her now making her final journey instead of his sister. Such a thought provided no comfort at all, and he cursed himself for even thinking it.

If there was one overwhelming feeling that was increasingly beginning to engulf the farmer, however, it was the sense of vulnerability that the recent burglary, and now the murder on his premises, had stirred up. As a lone resident in a large house with too many rooms for his needs, a growing siege mentality was increasingly beginning to grow within him. Twice in three months his home had been violated. He could not protect himself or those whom he loved. On top of that, the perpetrator may very well be residing just a few hundred yards from his house. As each day passed, he became further convinced that his ploughman had had a hand in the proceedings.

Some three quarters of an hour later the coffin was taken within the old kirk. Henderson barely noticed as the minister gave the sermon, his grief now having utterly consumed him. As her casket was later taken outside in the midst of a light shower and lowered into a grave, his mind lingered over the fact that with the death of his beloved sister, another part of him was now also forever lost.

As the Mount Stewart murderer remained at large, another killer continued to move silently and unchecked throughout the countryside around Perth. Despite the control orders banning the movement of livestock across the county, the rinderpest virus was still continuing to breach parochial defences with deadly effect. In Coupar Angus, twenty-one animals were slaughtered; in Carse, some thirty-five animals were also culled. It was well known that the rinderpest virus could not be transmitted to humans, but the idea of a contamination of the everyday environment was a deeply depressing affair. Many amongst the farming community continued to believe that they had to rely on prayer as much as on science to resolve the situation.

With each printed edition of the newspapers came new facts and considered speculation about the Mount Stewart Murder, as it was now being called. Much of these were transformed into wild rumours that spread faster than any plague. Some believed that William Henderson had killed his sister. When questioned as to why the man would murder his sibling in such a way, the conversation would dwell on the inherent wickedness with which the farmer himself must have been infected. For others in the county, Henderson was clearly an innocent man, the unfortunate victim of circumstances, and someone to be pitied rather than persecuted.

The strangest rumours were those that did not involve Mount Stewart Farm at all. A man in a house near Perth was said to have murdered his wife through the administration of poison. A child residing in Bridgend had been killed by his father; whilst in the city's Meal Vennel there were so many tales of murders being committed that the humble traveller may well have been wise to avoid the narrow lane for the time being altogether. The press noted the spread of the rumours as much as the actual facts, with the *Perthshire Advertiser* later describing the verbal labours of the masses as being 'the product of some over-heated brain, or the wilful falsehoods of some lover of horrible tales'.

On Friday, 6 April, Chief Constable Gordon and the procurator fiscal held a meeting in constabulary headquarters to discuss the progress of the investigation so far. William Henderson was no longer considered to be a suspect but there were still questions over Crichton's whereabouts on Friday, 30 March. Had he been working away from the farm for the whole day? Did he change his clothes between the morning and the afternoon, and if so, why? Equally important was the identity of the mysterious man observed by Betsy Riley talking to the victim at midday, just hours before her death. Was he the same man that had been seen by Crichton at about three o'clock in the afternoon? The description given was so vague that it was impossible to tell. And had Crichton also witnessed somebody else at the farm at eleven o'clock, as he was stated to have told William Henderson and James Rogers, but later denied?

While Janet Rogers was being buried in Auchtergaven, the fiscal and the two detectives had travelled to the Bridge of Earn police station to interview Crichton's neighbours, James Barlas, his wife Jean Hally, and son Robert. The mason had been at work on the day of the murder at the Moncreiffe Tunnel, and could offer little testimony beyond his involvement in the discovery of the victim's body. He did claim, however, that he had witnessed Crichton on a couple of occasions smoking at mealtimes, though never in his own cottage. In discussing Henderson's relationship with his servants, the mason confirmed that he was said to have a reputation locally for his 'lubidious propensities'.

The only other observation that the mason could offer was that he had seen a pair of Crichton's trousers bleaching on the grass in front of his house on the day after the murder. The mason's wife had been able to offer little also. She had travelled to Perth in the late morning of the killing, though had been at Linnlea when Betsy Riley had come hawking her wares; indeed, she had bought a small jug from the woman.

Fifteen-year-old Robert Barlas had been working in the garden of the cottage for much of the day. At about three o'clock in the afternoon he had also observed a gentleman walking across a field beside the farm. The stranger had been dressed in a dark round-tailed coat and cloth trousers, and had worn a cloth bonnet with a snout. He had seemed quite elderly and had taken a good half an hour to reach the track beside the cottages at Linnlea; the lad assumed he had been making for the main road into Forgandenny or Dunning. Beyond that the boy could offer no further help, though he did add that he had not seen anybody in the vicinity either at eleven o'clock or midday. His observance of a man near the farm in the middle of the afternoon seemed to confirm James Crichton's testimony on the same matter.

Edinburgh's Detective Officer James Leadbetter had now been with the Perthshire county police force for two days. In that time he had had ample opportunity to visit the crime scene and to examine all of the statements and evidence gathered so far. When asked for his opinion as to whether any further angle had yet to be covered, he replied that all possible leads that he could see were being adequately followed. As such, he believed that he would be unable to offer any further assistance, and so would be returning to the capital later that day. He suggested that the one option that was still open to the chief constable and the fiscal was the offer of a pecuniary reward to the public for further information. The idea was wholeheartedly agreed upon, and the detective was subsequently thanked for his presence and expert insight into the case.

————·——

The nervousness of Perth's residents was further exacerbated on Sunday, 8 April, with news of yet another murder – this time within the city itself.

On the previous evening two officers of the City Police Force had escorted an intoxicated rope spinner by the name of William Scott back to his father's property at Guthrie's Close, located within the Kirkgate, a small street leading off from the north of St John's Kirk. Following the constables' departure the father, a tannery labourer named Charles Scott, had rowed with his son and in the process had assaulted him in the house, the beating having only stopped when his wife had intervened. William had fallen to the ground during the assault with a bleeding head, and his mother had managed to place him in his bed to recover. Not long after, both of his parents had left the house, with each independently finding their way to a bottle. Witnesses had then described how the couple had continued to row drunkenly throughout the night upon their return home.

It was not until six o'clock on the Sunday morning that it became clear that the situation had deteriorated considerably. Charles Scott had called on a neighbour for assistance, claiming that his wife had died in the night, and had asked her to accompany him to dress her corpse. The terrified neighbour had refused, forcing Scott to make his way to his daughter's house in Craigie, about a mile away to the east of the town, to inform her that her mother was dead. By the time the pair had returned to Scott's house in the Kirkgate, a crowd had gathered; at this point the tanner was forced to alert the City Police Force of the death of his wife.

Officers rapidly made their way to the house, along with the force's surgeon. Inside they found the woman in her bed, clearly deceased and with a large wound to the back of her head. Both father and son were promptly arrested on suspicion of murder, despite the tanner's assertions that she had fallen out of the bed during the night and injured herself in the process. The Perth crowd had been greatly excited by the proceedings, loitering around the Kirkgate for most of the day, their numbers swelled by those who had travelled to the kirk to worship. Those unfamiliar with the story immediately assumed that the Forgandenny killer had claimed his second victim. It was soon determined that the young William Scott had taken no part in the apparent killing. His father most certainly had a case to answer for, and was duly lodged in the county prison building.

The public was quickly reassured that a suspect for this latest atrocity was now under lock and key, and awaiting trial. The Mount Stewart murderer, however, would not be so easily identified and detained.

SEVEN

MANHUNT

The Lord Advocate's office in Edinburgh readily agreed to the idea of offering a reward in the Mount Stewart investigation. A sum of £100 was authorised, to be paid 'to any person who shall forthwith give such information to the Procurator Fiscal of Perthshire, or to the Chief Constable of County Police at Perth, as shall lead to the conviction of the Murderer'.

News of the reward was published within the county's newspapers and in a further handbill entitled 'Murder: Revised Information', which also carried details of the recently discovered missing items of clothing from William Henderson's farm. It was now suspected that the missing items had been stolen in order to allow the killer to change out of the bloody garments, which must surely have been created by such a vicious assault. With a new push for information from the public now underway, the constabulary's workload was about to dramatically increase.

On Tuesday, 10 April, the constabulary was contacted by a member of the public, who brought news of a gentleman by the name of Simpson who had been seen on the previous day travelling to Dundee, and dressed in clothing heavily stained by blood. The authorities in the city were quickly contacted and agreed to arrest the man, whilst a constable was dispatched from Perth to bring him back to the town for questioning. In the ensuing investigation, Simpson protested that he was a cattle drover who had been employed to slaughter sheep in a village in the county on the previous day. It was for this reason, he claimed, that his vest bore so much blood. Betsy Riley was again called out to identify a potential suspect, but was once more unable to do so. The drover was detained overnight and then released early the next day by the order of the procurator fiscal.

Several similar sightings were received from across the country over the course of the following week, the news of the reward having excited the aspirations of many fortune hunters across the land. Further requests were also received from forces across the country seeking additional clarification on the descriptions as given in the bills. In one bizarre enquiry, Superintendent McDonald received a message from the police force in Stirling. In this he was advised that a suspect had been arrested in connection with the murder, in a public house on the road from Falkirk to the town. The gentleman's name was Charles McDonald, a native of the Isle of Skye. After indulging in some refreshments, the islander had asked the landlord if he had ever heard of the murder at Mount Stewart Farm. The landlord replied that it had been well discussed in the area, at which stage the drunken man had then boasted that both he and an accomplice were both being hunted down by the police for having committed the crime. As he continued to drink the landlord had managed to summon the local constable, who then arrested McDonald and took him to the cells at Stirling police station. His description was found in no way to have matched that given by Betsy Riley, but the Stirling force had felt it prudent to confirm with the Perthshire force if it had been searching for the man. After the superintendent had sent a telegram back saying that they had not been looking for a Charles McDonald, the islander was freed.

Many such enquiries were received by McDonald and his men, and each had to be dealt with. Far from flushing out the murderer, the prospect of the reward was instead adding considerable weight to the constabulary's already heavy workload.

———•———

On the morning of Monday, 16 April, Superintendent McDonald was handed a telegram which had been sent to the procurator fiscal's office. The message had been sent on behalf of Superintendent Ian Duthie of the city police force in Aberdeen, and described the detention in the city of a travelling hatter by the name of John Henderson. As with many others, he had appeared to match the description being circulated.

As luck would have it, an officer of the Aberdeen force was in the Perth County Constabulary office that day on another matter. Rather than send a telegram, McDonald asked the young constable to take a written response back to the city with him upon his return that afternoon. In the letter the superintendent requested that a detailed description of Henderson be given, as well as an exact account of what the gentleman might have to say about his whereabouts on the day of the murder, in order that the truth of his statement could be tested. A reply was received at noon on the following day, which stated that the arrested man was claiming to be unsure about his whereabouts on the day of the killing. Unsatisfied with his answer, arrangements were duly made for him to be brought to Perth.

Late on the Tuesday evening John Henderson was brought from Aberdeen to Perth railway station, and taken into custody by Sergeant Charles Ross. The smell coming from the prisoner suggested that he had certainly been the worse for drink on the previous day, prior to his arrest. The Aberdonian constable who had conveyed him to the city had informed Ross that the hatter had been protesting his innocence ever since his detention. The sergeant thanked him and then instructed the hatter to hold his tongue until he could be formally questioned at the police station.

It was now dark, the sun having just set. The main interior of the constabulary's headquarters was lit only by a solitary gas lamp, whilst a single candle barely illuminated the superintendent's office. Henderson was taken into the building and asked to provide some basic details to the duty constable, such as his name, age, occupation and present residential address in Aberdeen. As he did so, he informed the policeman that he was married to a woman whose surname was Rogers; a coincidence that the press would undoubtedly have a field day with once discovered. The hatter's coat pockets were then emptied to reveal several small everyday items, including a ticket from a pawn shop in Aberdeen. When asked what had been pawned, Henderson stated that he had been forced to trade in some items of clothing, as he had been somewhat straitened financially.

Despite the fact that it was so late in the evening, Betsy Riley was sent for from her house in South Street. Although angry at having been disturbed once again by the police, she agreed to be taken to the High Street premises. Arriving a few minutes later, she was brought before the suspect in the superintendent's office. McDonald asked her to take a good look at the man now in front of her.

'Betsy, is this the man that you saw at Mount Stewart Farm on the day of the murder of Mrs Rogers?' he asked.

At this the hatter tried to stand up to again protest his innocence, but was immediately seated by one of the constables behind him.

'I was nowhere near the area at the time of that woman's death. I was in Edinburgh on that day,' he exclaimed loudly. 'I keep telling you man, I've not been in Perth or anywhere near here for months, if not longer.'

'Mr Henderson, we will be questioning you as to your exact whereabouts on the day in due course,' Sergeant Ross intervened. 'In the meantime sir, you will please remain silent, until you are requested to speak.'

The Irish hawker stepped towards the suspect and walked around him, trying to make out his features in the flickering light of the candle's flame. The man certainly had a long face and whiskers, and appeared to be middle-aged, but the Irishwoman claimed that it was difficult to make out his features properly with so little light.

'It is hard to say now Mr McDonald, sir,' she stated, squinting at the man before her. 'It might well be him and it might just as well not be. I wouldn't wish to be saying it isn't if it might be, if you get my meaning.'

'Mrs Riley,' the superintendent interrupted, 'it has been a long day and my patience is being sorely tried. Can you tell me whether this is or is not the man that you saw at the farm?'

Clearly irritated by his tone, Betsy turned from the suspect and strode over to the superintendent with a look of indignation. 'Well how am I supposed to be saying if this is definitely the man that I saw if I can barely see him? I am not going to say it is him just to suit your impatience Mr McDonald, sir,' she said, waving a finger at him.

At this the sergeant shouted at the hawker to mind her tongue, for this was the deputy chief constable of the force that she was talking to – a night in the cells could easily be arranged if she so desired. A look of panic suddenly gripped Betsy's face, and, stepping back from the superintendent, she rapidly apologised for her manner.

Conceding that the room was quite dark, a tired McDonald instructed her to return back to the office at eight o'clock the next morning. As she left, he asked her not to share news of the arrest with anyone, though with little trust that she would actually listen. Following her departure he then gave the instruction for the still protesting Henderson to be taken to the cells next door and locked up for the night.

———

Early on Wednesday morning the superintendent arrived at the City Police Office to question the hatter further. As he had feared, the hawker had feasted well upon her release the previous evening within the local taverns, with several reporters now waiting at the door of the building. The policeman pushed his way through, ignoring their fevered questions, and made his way inside as one of the city constables closed the door after him.

Inside the building he found that John Henderson had already been awakened and fed. A commotion outside the building then signaled what could only be the arrival of Betsy Riley. The hawker was brought inside and the hatter fetched from his cell.

'Now Betsy, I will ask again,' started the superintendent, pointing to the seated hatter, 'is this the man that you saw at Mount Stewart Farm on Friday 30th March?'

In the full light of day the suspect's features were much clearer to see. His hair was unkempt and there was a few days' growth on his face. As the hawker approached him to have another look, she suddenly stopped and recoiled in apparent horror.

'Oh Lord have mercy, sir,' she exclaimed. 'That's him Mr McDonald, sir. That's the blackguard.'

'Are you absolutely sure Betsy?'

'Oh sir, that's him. He's the killer, sir, that's the man that I saw at Mount Stewart.'

'I'm no killer, ye crazy witch,' the hatter screamed at her indignantly. 'I don't know who she thinks I am, Mr Superintendent, sir. I haven't been near any bloody farm. I haven't even been in the county for months.'

The hawker stepped back, wailing now in horror. 'Keep him away from me, sir. Oh sweet Mary sir, it's the killer, keep him away.'

The superintendent told the woman to pull herself together, reminding her that even if this was the man who had been at the farm, it did not necessarily mean that he was the killer. The instruction was then given to take Henderson back to his cell. The merchant did not go quietly, vehemently protesting his innocence yet further as he was led away. With the hatter removed, McDonald asked the hawker again if she was absolutely certain that it was him.

'As God is my witness sir, that is him. I'm convinced of it,' she replied with conviction.

McDonald informed her that she would be required to confirm her identification in the presence of the fiscal. Knowing full well that as soon as she stepped out of the door the press would have a field day with her, the big Irishman further instructed that she be taken into a side room for the time being. At least here she would keep her tongue silent long enough for him to relay developments to the chief constable and the procurator fiscal. As the woman was escorted from the room, Sergeant Ross turned to his superior with a look of relief on his face.

'It looks like we might have him sir. The woman seems fair certain that it's him.'

'Aye, she is that,' he replied, with a note of doubt in his voice. 'I will inform Mr Gordon and Mr McLean. Stay here and keep the reporters out. They will undoubtedly be wishing to speak with the woman.'

McDonald walked to the door, but before exiting stopped and once more addressed his sergeant. 'At the moment, Charles, we have a suspect in custody. Let us not raise our hopes just yet.'

'Yes sir. Understood,' replied Ross, as the superintendent left the room.

———•———

At constabulary headquarters Chief Constable Gordon was finalising a copy of his first quarterly report of the year for the Police Committee. Following a knock on his door, McDonald stepped into his superior's office and informed him that Riley had made a positive identification of a suspect in the murder case. Gordon beckoned his deputy to take a seat. As he did so, the superintendent confirmed that the suspect did fit the description as circulated, but then added that he was unsure of the woman's evidence.

'On what basis do you doubt the woman, Henry?' enquired Gordon.

'Sir, when Riley was first brought in for questioning, just after the murder occurred, she made merry with the press over it, and was the talk of the whole town. The woman likes an audience, sir. Her husband is quite ill, and now that there is a reward on offer, I cannot help but think that she may have another motive here.'

'Do you believe she has been spinning us a yarn?' asked Gordon.

'It's quite possible, sir.'

Gordon thanked him for sharing his concern, but added that until they could prove otherwise they would have to take the woman's evidence at face value.

Within half an hour John McLean arrived at the office, accompanied by Sheriff Barclay, at which point McDonald led the party next door to the City Police Office cells. The suspect was again brought forward from his confinement, and this time examined by McLean, who invited him to explain his whereabouts on the day of the murder. Henderson replied that he had been in Edinburgh, selling various items of clothing for several days before and after the day of the murder. When asked where he had stayed, the hatter provided a list of inns, as well as the names of witnesses who could corroborate his presence there. He was again asked forensically to describe his movements both at the time of the murder and in the days after, to which he gave confident answers. During the questioning, however, he also let it slip that he had recently been imprisoned for a short period following an assault charge.

Riley was brought back in to confirm her identification of the man. She did so once more, but remarked that not only was he the man that she had seen at the farm, she now recalled that she had seen him elsewhere about the town of Perth itself, despite the hatter's denials of having been in the area for many months.

Following the questioning, the chief constable and the fiscal conferred briefly with the sheriff substitute in an adjacent room. The man was adamant that he had been in Edinburgh, and had listed several potential witnesses. These had to be investigated urgently. Due to the importance of the task at hand, McLean suggested that Gordon should personally travel to Edinburgh to follow up on the leads himself, to Barclay's approval.

If Riley was right, and John Henderson was the killer, the investigation would soon be brought to a close.

———

George Gordon travelled to Edinburgh by train on the Thursday morning, accompanied by Sergeant Ross. The City of Edinburgh police force had been given prior warning and had promised to co-operate in any way that it could. James Leadbetter greeted the two men at the city's Waverley Station and agreed to act as a liaison to help with their enquiries in the district.

Back in Perth, McDonald continued with his investigation at constabulary headquarters. Following Riley's identification of the man in front of the fiscal, the superintendent had sent a letter to his Aberdeen-based counterpart, Superintendent Duthie. Henderson had held a pawn ticket in his possession and McDonald wanted to know what had been exchanged for money. He requested that the items be retrieved from the pawn shop in Aberdeen and posted to him in a parcel, to see if they could be identified – the suspicion being that these might have been the clothes stolen from William Henderson. If the clothes were retained in Perth as a consequence of a positive identification, the pawnbroker would be duly compensated; if not, they would be sent back and the ticket returned to Henderson.

The letter found its intended recipient, and a reply was dispatched to Perth early on the Thursday morning. McDonald was advised that there would be a delay in retrieving the items from the pawnbroker's shop, as the owner was at present not within the city, and would not be returning for a few days. Until the package could be examined, and Henderson's alibis in Edinburgh confirmed, the hatter would have to remain in the cell.

McDonald continued to harbour doubts about Riley's identification of the man. Had she really seen him, or was the woman playing them all for fools? Were they placing too much reliance on her as a witness? Over the last three weeks the force had expended considerable manpower pursuing suspects from as far afield as Aberdeen and Dundee, solely on the basis of her testimony. With every arrest, the superintendent's misgivings continued to develop over her sincerity and integrity.

Unsurprisingly, the local newspapers were filled with details of John Henderson's detention. A couple of titles had noted their surprise that the hatter had not yet been freed, as had been the case with previous arrests in the case; they had taken this as evidence that the killer might indeed have been caught. McDonald was pleased to note that the *Perthshire Advertiser* had taken a more cautious line, describing how despite the proverb of 'murder will out', it was slow in coming in this case, with the investigation still shrouded in darkness almost three weeks on from the killing. The rest of the article, however, was about to add further pressure to the constabulary's already struggling efforts.

The newspaper had printed a letter written by the victim's widower, James Rogers, which had been submitted to its offices at the beginning of the week. Clearly troubled by the rumours surrounding his brother-in-law's alleged involvement in the murder, and the slow pace of the investigation, the labourer had felt that he should speak out. In a heartfelt account, he described his own experience of the terrible event and his encounters with the farmer in its immediate aftermath. More importantly for McDonald, Rogers made it equally clear that he was lacking confidence in the constabulary's efforts to date.

The labourer started by outlining how he had been informed of his wife's killing whilst at work in the woods of Rohallion, and how he had made his way to Mount Stewart Farm to discover that the reports had been true. He then turned to the main purpose of his piece, to show that it categorically could not have been committed by William Henderson:

> Now for the murderer. What was his motive? Evidently plunder, as lockfasts had been torn off, and all parts of the house rifled. Was there energy on the part of the authorities to detect the murderer and thief, or was there a facility given for his escape? I have my doubts. It is evident from what my brother-in-law tells me, that some months previous his house was broken into by a window, a silver watch and £2-worth of money carried off, besides a pair of trousers, the trousers being got some days after, lying in that belt of wood running along the north side of the steading. The robbery was reported to the police of the district, the number of the watch given, but no clue was ever found to this case. I have a strong impression on my mind that the depredator of the first case has been the murderer in the second; had the first been found out, the second might have been prevented.
>
> Two police kept a close watch over the house and its inmates till up to Sunday afternoon, until one of their supervisors arrived from Perth, and

dispersed them among the neighbourhood farm-steads and villages to seek for information. I evidently saw that their suspicion up to this time related on the innocent. This suspicion, by using sound logic, might have been thrown to the wind at the first stage of examination, which I can show. On examining the ploughman on Monday morning, he told me that he saw Mrs Rogers at the kitchen door talking to a man through the course of the day. This shows that she was alive after her brother left for Perth. He likewise told me that they unharnessed their horses both together at night, and he left his master in the stable. Now, it was impossible that he could have committed such an unnatural, heartrending deed, and put the house in the state it was found in, between that time and the time he gave the alarm. Besides, she was his favourite member of the family, one whom he always opened his mind to. I will never forget his cries on Sunday morning. He took me aside from the house, and gave vent to his grief in cries most pitiful.

I can assure the public, who have been listening to many a wild rumour these two weeks past, that there is not the least shadow of suspicion resting on my mind, or on the minds of any of Mr Henderson's friends, concerning this foul deed.

JAMES ROGERS - Airntully, April 16, 1866.

The constabulary was convinced that William Henderson was nothing more than a tragic victim of a horrendous crime, his innocence beyond question. In that regard McDonald sincerely hoped that Rogers' intervention would be useful in taking pressure off the farmer. The stinging condemnation vented against the constabulary by the widower would, however, only add further pressure to its efforts. McDonald desperately hoped that they could wrap up the investigation as quickly as possible.

To complicate matters further, McDonald was now informed of the arrest of yet another suspect, once again in Dundee. An Irish dealer in old clothes by the name of Collins had been detained that morning on suspicion of being the murderer, his description also being said to have matched that currently circulating in the handbills. As with Simpson a few days before, he was brought by train to Perth just after midday and taken before the procurator fiscal. Betsy Riley was once more asked to identify him, and immediately declared that she had never seen the man before, asserting that the man who had been at the farm was now seated in the city cells. Any further arrests, she insisted, would be completely pointless. With no reason to detain him further, an incensed Collins was released after just a couple of hours and allowed to return to Dundee.

Pondering over the hatter's testimony in the cells from the previous day, McDonald surmised that if he had indeed travelled to Perth in the recent past to sell items of clothing, as now claimed by Riley, some other person in the town must have had dealings with him professionally. It was also likely that he must have stayed in one of the city's lodging houses. If the woman was being truthful with her evidence then the man must have been seen. There was only one way to find out, he decided – it was time to stir up the locals.

Putting on his coat, McDonald instructed one of his constables to fetch John Cameron from the fiscal's office. He gave further orders to have Henderson brought from his cell in the City Police Office next door. The man was to be brought back into the County Constabulary office and kept under guard. The superintendent then advised all in the office to get ready to receive some visitors – a lot of visitors.

With the arrival of Cameron, McDonald strode out of the building and into a heavy shower of rain, which had just commenced. He walked along the High Street and rapped hard on the door of every lodging house that could be found, carrying on his efforts with all of the main streets of the small city centre. At each door he respectfully asked the keeper to spare just five or ten minutes to make his or her way towards the County Constabulary headquarters, as he had a suspect that he wished for them to look at. Some who resided just doors away from each other walked together in groups towards the building. Those who protested that it was pouring with rain were told to bring an umbrella, put on a coat or enjoy God's own gift to the soil, but they were to proceed with haste to the office nevertheless. As well as the lodging house keepers, the superintendent and the criminal officer also approached any clothing merchants that they encountered on their path, asking them to spare a few moments also.

For the rest of the afternoon a regular procession of individuals turned up at the police office to take a good look at John Henderson's face. Most immediately stated that they had never seen him before, with one or two at first unsure but then coming to the conclusion also that they too had not. As one person left the tenement building, another would step in, with the constables doing their best to coordinate the sudden migration of Perth's inhabitants into their office.

The activity continued for almost four hours before the superintendent concluded that they must have approached most, if not all, of those who could in any way have had any dealings with the man. As McDonald feared, not a single person had ever laid eyes on him.

—–·—–

At eight o'clock in the evening, the exhausted superintendent returned to his home at 48 South Methven Street, to be greeted by his wife, Margaret, who had already dined that evening with their children. As she prepared to put out a meal for her husband, a loud knock was suddenly heard at the door. On rushing to answer, Margaret was surprised to find Sergeant Ross standing outside in the rain. He apologised for disturbing her at such a late hour, but requested to speak to the superintendent immediately. The rain-soaked officer was quickly brought in and after removing his coat was asked to step into the drawing room, while Margaret fetched her husband.

'Good evening, Charles. This is quite a late hour to be calling,' observed the superintendent, as he entered the room. 'How was your trip to Edinburgh?'

'My apologies sir, we have only just returned. Mr Gordon has asked me to inform you of what we found. I'm afraid it is not good news.'

The superintendent invited the sergeant to take a seat, and asked him if he required any refreshment. He declined, at which point McDonald asked his wife to let them have the room. With the door closed, the sergeant was asked to share what had been discovered.

'Well sir, Mr Gordon and I met up with Mr Leadbetter, as arranged, and we spent most of the day visiting various taverns within the city centre to ask the proprietors if they had ever heard of Henderson.'

'And how did you fare?' asked McDonald.

'I'm afraid we established fairly quickly that he was very well known in the area,' replied the sergeant. 'It would appear, sir, that the man is telling the truth. At the time of the murder he had already been in Edinburgh for a few days. We spoke to several witnesses who can testify to the fact, and that he was completely drunk on the day of the murder itself.'

McDonald's expression darkened as he reflected on the findings. 'Does he have an alibi for the whole day, Charles?' he asked, though already suspecting the answer.

'I'm sorry sir, but yes. He was drunk from the day before and for much of the following day also. He had apparently made quite a few sales earlier in the week, and spent the rest of the week drinking his profits.'

A furious McDonald slammed his fist heavily onto the table beside him. 'I knew it Charles. That damnable woman Riley has been lying to us all along.'

'It would appear so, sir. I'm sorry, sir – you were clearly right to be cautious.'

The implications were clear. If John Henderson had a cast-iron alibi, then Riley had either deliberately or mistakenly identified him as having been at Mount Stewart. Whilst it seemed that she had led the force on a merry dance for the last few days, more worrying now was the possibility that her entire testimony was completely fabricated.

EIGHT

THE BLAIRINGONE KILLER

The discoveries in Edinburgh had now completely blown apart the strategy that Chief Constable Gordon had been pursuing for the last month in the Mount Stewart case. Upon his return to Perth he had informed both Sheriff Barclay and Procurator Fiscal McLean of the development, and a review of the case to date had been urgently implemented by the two gentlemen. The decision was taken that a mere description of any prospective suspects matching that given by Betsy Riley would no longer be enough to warrant an arrest; additional concrete evidence was now required.

The hawker was not entirely ruled out as a witness to the investigation. Although her assertion that John Henderson was the man she had witnessed at Mount Stewart Farm had now been so dramatically disproved, it was still unclear as to whether she had in fact lied about the original description, or indeed if she had seen anybody at the farm on the day in question at all. It had, after all, been offered to the force before any word of a reward had been announced, and only hours after the killing had taken place. The police had sought Riley out; she had not approached them. Her effectiveness as a witness who could potentially testify in a court of law was nevertheless becoming more doubtful.

The final confirmation of John Henderson's innocence had arrived at the constabulary headquarters on the Monday morning, with the delivery of a package addressed to Superintendent McDonald. Once opened it was discovered to contain John Henderson's pawn ticket and several items of clothing that had been retrieved from the pawnbroker's shop in Aberdeen. All of the items were clearly new materials designed for sale by a travelling salesman, with none presenting the appearance of ever having been worn.

They were certainly not the clothes that had been stolen from William Henderson's bedroom.

The hatter had finally been released early in the morning of Tuesday, 23 April, after almost a week's detention. For the inconvenience of his detention he was offered sixteen shillings as compensation. Henderson had complained that the amount was woefully inadequate for the horrendous ordeal that he had endured, a position that the journalists gathered outside the cells waiting for him to emerge were only too happy to agree with.

Gordon was becoming increasingly concerned about the press. In recent months there had been a dramatic escalation in the number of murders across Britain. With each new investigation, journalists had been asking increasingly difficult questions of those tasked with solving them. The increase in the murder rate, the methods for such investigations, and the punishments administered to those found guilty were now debated almost daily within the nation's newspapers. As with James Rogers' recent letter, many journalists were now also openly asking questions of the Mount Stewart investigation.

In the *Dundee Courier and Argus* of Wednesday, 18 April, an article entitled 'The Recent Murders' had suggested that the use of corporal punishment in deterring future murders was counter-productive. This was particularly so, it claimed, when applied to a certain class of criminal mind, where 'the depravity of such criminals had gone so far and become so deep that the story of other crimes, and even that of the condign punishment of their perpetrators, may act as a frightful charm or incentive for them to fill up the measure of their own criminality'. This possibility, the paper opined, could well be the reason behind the increase in the murder rate. For every delivery to a jail, it suggested, there appeared to be the perpetration of yet another atrocious crime.

This was blatantly the situation with three recent examples where the killers had so far escaped apprehension. The Mount Stewart Murder was one case, the other two being the killing of a housekeeper in London called Millson and the recent tragedy surrounding a young girl called Melvin, who had been murdered in Gateshead. The paper noted that 'in none of these cases has there any clue been got to the murderers; suspicion has either been at fault, or has not found any circumstances to give it a personal direction'.

The writer had then attacked the police handling of such investigations. It could not but be felt to be desirable, it stated, that 'the detective department of the police service possessed some part of the genius with which detectives officers are commonly endowed in the pages of fiction', a quality seemingly

The farmhouse as sketched on the day after the murder by architect David Smart – note the ladder used by William Henderson to gain entry. (National Records of Scotland, RHP141081-1)

William Henderson finds Janet's body. (Illustration by Garry Walton, *Your Family Tree* Issue 43, Autumn 2006, ©Future Publishing)

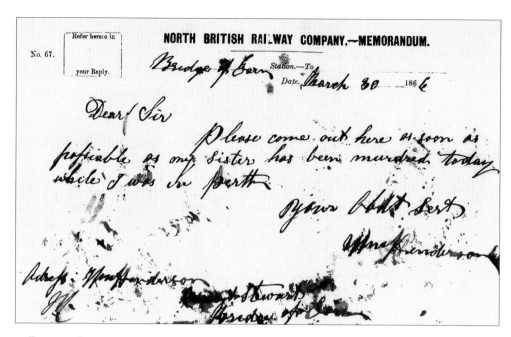

William Henderson's urgent note to the procurator fiscal of Perth, shortly after finding Janet's body. (National Records of Scotland, JC26/1867/20)

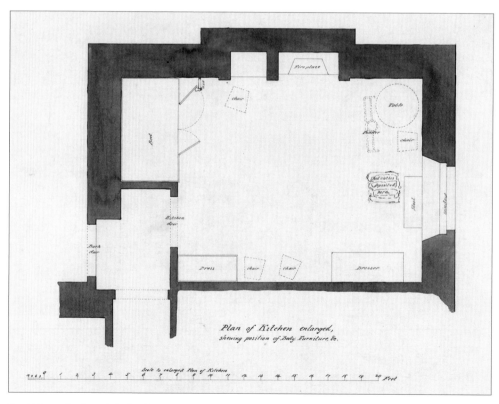

David Smart's plan of the kitchen at Mount Stewart, showing the location of the bedclothes under which the body was found, and the kitchen axe. (National Records of Scotland, RHP141081-1)

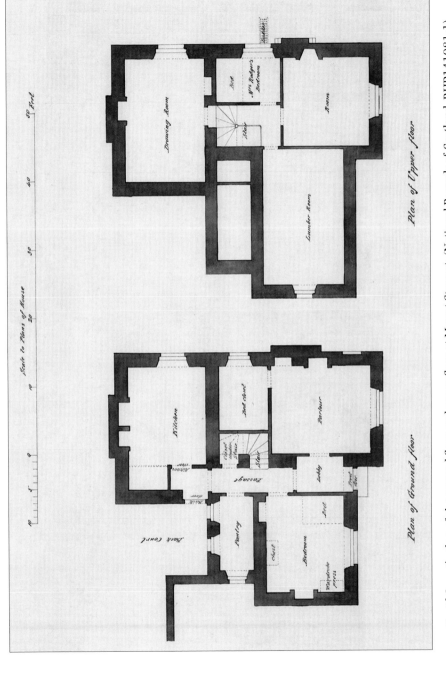

Plan of Upper floor

Plan of Ground floor

David Smart's plan of the ground floor and upper floor at Mount Stewart. (National Records of Scotland, RHP141081-1)

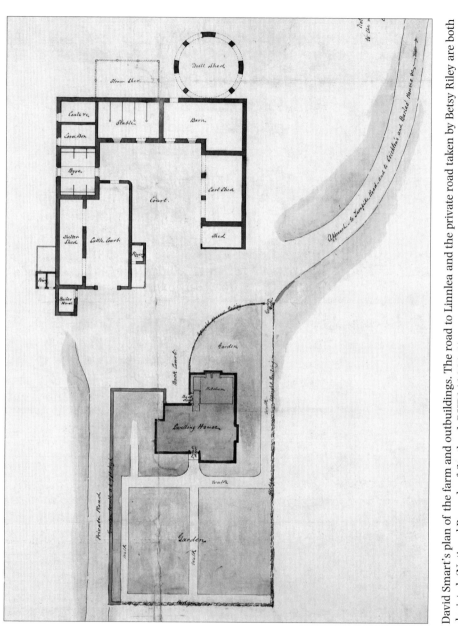

David Smart's plan of the farm and outbuildings. The road to Limnlea and the private road taken by Betsy Riley are both depicted. (National Records of Scotland, RHP141081-1)

MURDER.

DURING the day time on Friday, the 30th March last, JANET HENDERSON or ROGERS, was barbarously MURDERED in the Kitchen of the FARM HOUSE of MOUNT STEWART, in the Parish of Forgandenny, and County of Perth, by some person or persons at present unknown.

From the appearance of the Body and Furniture, in said House, their is every reason to believe that the party or parties who committed the said Crime, must have been considerably covered with blood.

With the exception of a LARGE OUTER-DOOR KEY, nothing has been missed from said house which can again be identified.

About Noon on said day, a man of the following description, supposed to be the Murderer, was seen at the Kitchen door of said house :—

> Between 40 and 50 years of age. About 5 feet 9 inches in height. Brown Hair, and Small Dark Whiskers. Long Face. Slender make, and thin in figure. Dressed in a dirty darkish Cap, Dark Frock-tailed Coat, rather long ; Grayish coloured Trousers. Rather Seedy appearance. Did not look like a working man. He is supposed to have had a small dog, of a dark or grayish colour, along with him.

It is earnestly requested that any information relative to the matter, may be immediately communicated to the Procurator Fiscal, or Chief Constable of County Police, at Perth, or to any Police Constable.

County Police Office,
PERTH, 4th April, 1866.

C. G. SIDEY, PRINTER, PERTH.

One of the first handbills printed describing Betsy Riley's suspect, wanted in connection with the murder. (National Records of Scotland, JC26/1867/20)

PROCLAMATION.

REWARD

OF

£100.

WHEREAS, during the day time, on Friday the 30th March last, JANET HENDERSON or ROGERS, was barbarously MURDERED, in the Kitchen of the Farm House of MOUNT STEWART, in the Parish of Forgandenny, and County of Perth, by some person or persons at present unknown.

A REWARD OF

ONE HUNDRED POUNDS

is hereby offered by Government, to any Person who shall forthwith give such information to the Procurator Fiscal of Perthshire, or to the Chief Constable of County Police at Perth, as shall lead to the conviction of the Murderer.

Procurator Fiscal's Office,
PERTH, 10th April, 1866

C. G. SIDEY, PRINTER, PERTH.

Subsequent poster outlining details of the £100 reward. (National Records of Scotland, JC26/1867/20)

The Perth City Police Office, High Street, Perth, *c*.1878. (000-000-480-802-R © Perth Museum and Art Gallery. Licensor www.scran.ac.uk)

Right: Chief Constable George Gordon. (Courtesy of Tayside Police Museum)

Below: The police station at Sealsbank, Bridge of Earn. (000-000-488-509-R © Perth Museum and Art Gallery. Licensor www. scran.ac.uk)

The Murray Royal Hospital, date unknown. (Courtesy of Pamela Coventry)

Page 9.

Register of Corrected Entries

for the *Parish* of *Forgandenny*,

in the *County* of *Perth*

The following report of the result of a Precognition has been received touching the death of Janet Henderson or Roger Registered under No 4 in the Register Book of deaths for the year 1866

Name age and Sex	When and where died	Cause of Death
Janet Henderson or Rodger aged about 51 a female Perth 25th April 1867 Certified by J. young Pro P. Fiscal 1st August 1867 at Forgandenny Lindsay Bell Registrar	Between 10 Oclock morning and 7 Oclock evening of Friday the 30th March 1866 within the Farm house of Mount Stewart in the Parish of Forgandenny and Shire of Perth then Occupied by William Henderson Farmer	Injuries inflicted on the head by some one unknown As Certified by Dr. Laing Bridge of Earn and Abbots Perth who dissected body

The Register for Corrected Entries noting the cause of Janet's death as 'injuries inflicted on the head by someone unknown', following the trial in 1867. (By kind permission of the Registrar General for Scotland)

[Form A]

THE PETITION, STATEMENT, MEDICAL CERTIFICATES, SHERIFF'S ORDER, AND OBLIGATION,

Required for Admission of Patients into

The Murray Royal Asylum, Perth.

25 and 26 Vict., Cap. 54. Sect. 14.

PETITION TO THE SHERIFF TO GRANT ORDER FOR THE RECEPTION OF A PATIENT INTO THE MURRAY ROYAL ASYLUM, PERTH.

Unto the Honourable the (¹) *Sheriff* of the (²) *County* of *Perth* and his Substitutes,—

The Petition of *Melville Jameson* of *Perth, Solicitor* humbly sheweth that it appears from the subjoined Statement and accompanying Medical Certificates, that *William Henderson Belford Place New Scone* your Petitioner's (³) *Client* is at present in a state of Mental Derangement, a proper person for treatment in an Asylum for the Insane. May it therefore please your Lordship to authorize the transmission of the said *William Henderson* to the Murray Royal Asylum, Perth, and to sanction *his* admission into the said Asylum,

(Signed) *Melville Jameson*

Dated this (⁴) *Twentieth* day of *May* One thousand eight hundred and *eighty one*

STATEMENT.

If any of the Particulars in this Statement be not known, the fact to be so stated.

1. Christian Name and Surname of Patient at length, *William Henderson*
2. Sex and Age, *Male. 69 years*
3. Married, Single, or Widowed, *Single*
4. Condition of Life, and previous Occupation (if any), *Retired Farmer*
5. Religious Persuasion, so far as known, *Established Church*
6. Previous Place of Abode, *New Scone formerly Mount Stuart*
7. Place where Found and Examined, *New Scone*
8. Length of time Insane, *About ten days*
9. Whether First Attack, *Yes*
10. Age (if known) on First Attack, *69*
11. When and where previously under Examination and Treatment, *Never*
12. Duration of Existing Attack, *10 days*
13. Supposed Cause,
14. Whether subject to Epilepsy, *No*
15. Whether Suicidal,
16. Whether Dangerous to others,
17. Christian Name and Surname, and Place of Abode, of nearest known Relative of Patient, and degree of Relationship (if known), and whether any Member of the Family known to be or to have been Insane, *Mrs Isabella Henderson or Anderson, Murthly* *No*
18. Special circumstances (if any) preventing the insertion of any of the above particulars, *No*

I certify that, to the best of my knowledge, the above particulars are correctly stated.

Dated this *Twentieth* day of *May* One thousand eight hundred and *eighty one*

(To be signed by Person applying) *Melville Jameson*

Asylum record showing William's initial entry to the Murray Royal in 1881. (University of Dundee Archive Services, THB 29/8/2/10) found deficient beyond London. It further added that in many cases rural forces were so incapable of such work that they often had to hire in expertise from Glasgow and Edinburgh – as had happened recently with the Mount Stewart case.

The Edinburgh-based *Caledonian Mercury* had also put forth its views. In a piece on Thursday, 19 April, one of its writers had tried to ascertain whether there could be a common motive behind the spate of recent killings. Working its way through a list of such cases, it ended its inventory with the two recent murders in Perthshire. Of the woman Scott in Perth's Meal Vennel, it described the loss of life as to some extent still a mystery, but noted that a degree of domestic discomfort was clearly a factor. At Mount Stewart Farm, it surmised that plunder had been the motive. Taking into account a range of possibilities as to why the rate might be increasing, it asked if men and women were becoming increasingly wicked and less concerned about the most sacred of earthly things, such as life. Was society going back to the antediluvian era, or were such crimes simply becoming epidemical like cholera? It too concluded that 'hanging was no deterrent to crime' and that penal service was 'no bar to murderous outrage'.

Gordon shared the newspapers' opinion that the stakes had never been higher, but was in complete disagreement about their analysis of the situation. If murder truly was becoming an epidemic across Britain, then fire had to be fought with fire. Justice had not only to be served, but had to be seen to be served – its consequences had to be made highly visible to the public.

The suspect that the chief constable was convinced had been responsible for the murder of Alexander McEwan in December of the previous year was to be tried in Perth on 24 April. Gordon knew that the case being brought against the Englishman Joseph Bell, the so-called 'Blairingone Killer', was purely circumstantial in nature, but he was also aware that to keep the wolves at bay he and his force desperately needed a conviction.

The Circuit Court of Justiciary visited the city of Perth twice a year – in spring and autumn – to fulfill its longstanding obligations to deliver High Court justice across the country. The Spring Circuit was now underway, with the two judges presiding being Lords Ardmillan and Neaves. Both had already heard cases in Dundee during the previous week and were now accepting the hospitality of the Royal George Hotel in Perth.

Gordon was required to be present at the court in his capacity as chief constable of the three constabulary forces of Perthshire, Clackmannanshire and Kinross. With Superintendent McDonald and his other senior officers, he had accompanied their lordships on the first day of hearings as they had made their way towards the Sheriff Court. The opening of the court always attracted a degree of pomp and ceremony, and this year had been no different, with their lordships accompanied to the Sheriff Court by an escort troop of the 4th Hussars, a detachment of the County Constabulary and the band of the Perthshire Rifle Volunteers.

The first day of the court dealt with a range of cases, mainly theft related. Six of the culprits tried had been found guilty, with five given sentences of penal servitude. Today was now the second day of hearings, though the case of Joseph Bell was the only one scheduled to be heard. Being a trial for murder, a huge crowd had been drawn to the old Sheriff Court building. Those who could not get inside had remained in the vicinity for any scraps of news that could be gleaned from people coming and going from the proceedings.

Shortly after ten o'clock in the morning, the small courtroom was rapidly brought to order and the handcuffed defendant led into the dock. The twenty-eight-year-old poacher stood five foot eight inches in height, and although broad in build, his shoulders were stooped. He was well dressed in a dark shortcoat and trousers, the items clearly of a considerable age. Although his moustache was neatly trimmed, his eyes were bloodshot, as if from lack of sleep.

The indictment was read by the clerk of the court, and being asked how he wished to plead, Bell replied, 'Not guilty, my Lord,' in his broad Derbyshire accent. The Englishman was then seated, and the jury empanelled.

Opening the case for the prosecution, the Advocate Depute, James Arthur Crichton, first asked several witnesses to describe how the victim's body had been found. It was established that on the evening of 18 December 1865 a driverless horse and cart had been found near Vicker's Bridge, on the outskirts of Blairingone village, followed a few moments later by the sound of a gun being fired. A Perthshire constable, John Trotter, described how he had found a baker's van driver, Alexander McEwan, shortly afterwards at the side of the road, breathing his last.

The evidence then turned towards Bell's alleged involvement with a weaver called Robert Wright, describing how he had overheard the prisoner some ten days earlier discussing the method by which he had obtained the loan of a gun. The defence objected that such a statement could not possibly be relevant, but was overruled. Wright then recalled the defendant's chilling statement to him over a drink just two days before the murder – 'I know a man that comes from the Kinross side, and if you will catch the horse by the head, I will damned soon chuck him'. Bell had tried to claim subsequently that he was only joking, but the weaver had responded to say that he was not interested in that sort of thing.

A witness called Owen O'Hanlan further testified that he had seen Bell in the possession of a gun just two days before the murder. On the night of the killing the poacher had stayed at O'Hanlan's lodging house, and on the day after had asked his son to get his boots fixed, paying him a shilling to do so. Bell had also given a sum of money to one of his neighbours, claiming that he had had a good day's shooting the day before and could afford it.

At this stage the court turned to the investigation itself. It heard from another Perthshire constable, Peter Webster, who, having received intelligence to suggest the Englishman's involvement, had tracked him down and subsequently arrested him at a lodging house in Tillicoultry. The suspect had been escorted to Alloa Jail, and a search of his clothes had revealed a sizeable some of money. The superintendent of the Clackmannanshire force, Peter Chirnside, then explained how he had then taken the defendant's shoes to the scene of the crime and found the pattern to match that of footprints at the location.

A thirteen-year-old lad called James Kerr was next brought before the jury, and explained that he had found a gun in a small brook not far from Vicker's Bridge – believed to have been the murder weapon – which he had fished out of the water. At this point Chief Constable Gordon was briefly called to give evidence, to the effect that the gun that the boy had found was the same as the one he was now being shown in the courtroom.

On behalf of the prisoner a statement was then read to the court, outlining his account of himself as given before Sheriff Barclay on 25 December, shortly after his arrest. The poacher had not been able to identify where he had been at the time of the murder, though claimed he had been shooting on the day itself with a gun borrowed from a man in Collyland. He could not recall his name. The money in his possession was explained by the sale of fowl that he had shot to a man from Dunfermline, who had been in the area: again, he could not recall his name. Throughout the reading of the document, it was noted that Bell appeared to have an air of indifference about him.

With the conclusion of the statement, three game dealers from Dunfermline were then placed on the stand. Each denied having ever met Bell or of having purchased game from him. To the observant public, the weight of evidence against the potter turned poacher appeared to be growing heavier by the hour.

The counsel for the defence did not commence its evidence in support of Bell until seven o'clock in the evening, though by now the winds of fate were blowing ominously against him. The case was briefly adjourned for the night, to be reconvened by Lord Ardmillan on the following morning at ten o'clock.

When the trial resumed on Wednesday, 24 April, it was time to sum up the cases for both the prosecution and the defence. The Advocate Depute first gave a powerful speech on behalf of the prosecution to the jury, summarising the key points that surely pointed to the guilt of Joseph Bell. At the end of his address he advised the jury that, 'If you have a shadow of a doubt as to the guilt of the prisoner, I ask you to let him have the benefit of it.'

The case for the accused was then given by Bell's counsel, Mr Hall. In his opening remarks he apologised to the jury that the defence had had little by way of funds to support its client, which may have affected its portrayal of the case. It pointed out that Bell had claimed to have sold game to a dealer from Dunfermline, but had not named him. Was the appearance of just three such dealers from the town enough to conclusively prove that he had been lying about this? Would a poacher approach a respectable game dealer? Was it not entirely possible that a poacher of long standing such as Bell had actually simply done what he had indicated – borrowed a gun to poach game? Had any blood been observed on the defendant's clothing by those testifying to the court? Only one footprint had also been found at the scene of the crime, which had not been examined until two days after the murder. Could it really be so easy to say so definitively that it matched the shoe of Joseph Bell?

After an hour of vigorous and forensic rebuttal of the charge the defence then rested its case with one final appeal. 'The prisoner at the bar is a young man and in the course of nature has many years before him,' Hall stated, 'but your verdict, if it be not found in his favour, will close his career within a few days by an untimely and ignominious death.' In closing he added that, 'the evidence heard is altogether insufficient to justify you in taking any such course.'

With the summations concluded, Lord Ardmillan addressed the jury with the charge and a list of the facts as presented. The jurors then retired to consider their verdict, before returning just half an hour later with a decision. To Chief Constable Gordon's relief they found the case overwhelming against the poacher – the man was guilty as charged.

The consequences were now clear. The members of the public watched in fascination as the judge placed a black cap on his head, to pronounce the only sentence that the law could allow:

In respect of the verdict before recorded, Lords Ardmillan and Neaves discern and judge the panel, Joseph Bell, to be carried from the bar back to the prison of Perth, therein to be detained, and fed on bread and water only, till the 22nd of May next.

Upon that day, between the hours of eight and ten o'clock, we further ordain the said Joseph Bell to be taken from said prison to the common place of execution of the burgh of Perth, or to such place as the Magistrates of Perth shall appoint as a place of execution, and there, by the hands of the common executioner, be hanged by the neck upon a gibbet till he be dead.

Upon death his body will thereafter be buried within the precincts of the prison of Perth; and we further ordain his whole moveable goods and gear to be escheat and inbrought to her Majesty's use; which is pronounced for doom.

In concluding, his Lordship simply stated to the poacher, 'May God have mercy on your soul.'

The condemned man stood up and in a calm voice then said, 'Thank you my Lord, but I am innocent.'

Chief Constable Gordon and his men watched as the first man to be sentenced to death in Perth for seventeen years was led away. The verdict was correct; the judgement was sound. As things stood at the moment, however, he knew that it would be a considerable period of time before he might again return to the court to testify in similar circumstances against the Mount Stewart murderer.

NINE

A QUESTIONABLE WITNESS

With the publicity leading up to Joseph Bell's conviction casting light once more onto the Mount Stewart case, a new witness suddenly came forward.

Both James Crichton and Robert Barlas claimed to have seen a man walking across one of the fields by the farm at about three o'clock on the afternoon of the murder. At first it was considered that this might have been the same man witnessed by Betsy Riley earlier in the day. It now transpired that it was William Gormack, an elderly farmer residing within Forgandenny. The chronically ill seventy-nine-year-old man had left his farm at West Mill in order to look at a house at the back field of Dunbarney. He had set off shortly after three o'clock and had crossed the field towards Mount Stewart, taking about half an hour to do so. As he had approached the steading the old man had observed Crichton taking his horses from the stable and out to the field, where he had then harnessed them to a plough. He could not recall what the labourer had been wearing.

Gormack remembered that William Henderson's collie dog had been with the ploughman, as it had run over to him barking whilst he made his way through the farmyard. The animal had brushed past his leg and then run on to the kitchen door, where it had lain down. The door had been closed, he added, but he had no idea whether it was locked or not. There had been no reason to suspect that anything untoward might have happened in the building and so he had continued on his way down the track past the cottages at Linnlea. The only further observation that he could make was the fact that Crichton had returned to his work at quite a late time in the afternoon, whilst his master was away in Perth. He assumed that the labourer had merely taken some liberty with the situation. The old farmer also confirmed that William Henderson and his servant had barely been on speaking terms, and knew that Henderson had directly accused Crichton of the murder to his face.

Gormack's statement cast further doubt in the fiscal's mind over the reliability of the woman Riley's evidence. She may have heard that the old farmer had been in the area; perhaps she had even seen him herself? McLean directed the constabulary to determine whether everything that the woman claimed to have seen on the day could in fact fit into the chronology that she had given.

On Monday, 23 April, Constable Alexander Cumming was ordered to walk the length of the route which the hawker claimed to have travelled from the Bridge of Earn. He set off from his police station shortly after ten o'clock in the morning, and made his way along the road out of the village towards Forgandenny. Using a pocket notebook and a small, stubby pencil, the constable recorded exactly how long it took for the hawker to reach each of the places that she had stopped at, his pocket watch supplying the means to effectively time the different stages of her journey. Riley claimed to have had a break just outside of the village for a smoke, and true to the spirit of his task, the constable lifted out his own pipe to do likewise, before setting forth once more.

Cumming then proceeded to the Wright's house by the turn off for Pitkeathly Wells, and on to that of the shoemaker, pausing momentarily at each place to update his log, before turning onto the road leading up towards Mount Stewart Farm. At the two Linnlea cottages he then called into Mrs Barlas, and asked her to attend his police station on the following day, as Sergeant Ross wished to question her once more about her evidence. He bid her good day before continuing with his mission.

At the yard of Mount Stewart Farm, Henderson's dog ran up to the policeman, barking furiously and baring its teeth. It soon identified the stranger passing through and scurried away to the byre. The constable was careful to maintain the route which Riley claimed to have followed by the farmhouse, and made particular observation that the back door could be easily observed. He then continued past the farmyard and onto the path towards Dumbuils, and within minutes had reached the house of John and Mary Ritchie. A glance at his watch now revealed that the time was just a little after midday; the entire journey had taken him just over two hours. Whilst Betsy Riley's claims about what she had observed on the day of the murder were perhaps open to question, the timings she had given for her journey were exactly as she had described.

At Dumbuils Farm, the constable took the opportunity to question Mary Ritchie. The sixty-five-year-old farmer's wife stated that she had been washing in the house on the day of the murder from eight o'clock in the morning and had seen the hawker approach on the footpath through the two small windows of the wash house. Riley had only stopped at the farmhouse for a minute or two, and had said nothing about seeing any person outside Mount Stewart. Mary showed the constable the room where she had been working and pointed out that although she could not see the fields of Mount Stewart Farm, she did have a perfect view of the footpath. Nobody else had walked past her gaze on that day.

In order to carry out a more detailed investigation of James Crichton's movements on the day in question, Superintendent McDonald instructed his officers to speak to inhabitants of the farms adjacent to Mount Stewart. Although they had already been questioned, the first people to be examined about the ploughman's activities were Jean Barlas and her son Robert. James Barlas had noticed a pair of trousers bleaching on the grass the day after the murder; it stood to reason therefore that his wife and children may have witnessed Crichton's wife wash the items.

Constable Cameron asked Jean if she could recall any work having been carried out by Mrs Crichton on the day of the murder. The mason's wife answered by saying that upon her return from Perth, she had observed a tub standing at the door to the Crichton house, and remembered thinking that she must have been washing that day. This would have been at about five o'clock in the evening. She qualified her observation by adding that it was not unusual for Mrs Crichton to wash clothes on Fridays. Later in the evening, whilst making her way back down from the farmhouse, she had noticed that the tub was still beside her neighbour's doorway, but that on this occasion there had been items of men's clothing within it. This would have been after the discovery of the murder. Although pressed to describe what was in the tub, she stated that she could not positively remember whether the items were trousers, vests or coats. She saw nothing further that evening, for she had been terrified that the killer may still have been lurking within the vicinity, and had thus stayed inside the cottage with her husband and children. When asked if she had actually witnessed Mrs Crichton wash the items, Jean replied that she had not; she assumed the work had been done whilst she was in Perth.

Later in the evening Jean had spoken with both Crichton and his wife inside their cottage, the murder quite obviously drawing the focus of their discussions. The topic of washing had briefly arisen, but there had been no talk about the ploughman changing his clothes that day. Rather unusually, however, Crichton's wife had raised the subject with her a couple of weeks after the murder. She mentioned to the mason's wife that she was aware that her husband was being talked about as a possible suspect in the murder, simply because of his change in clothing. She explained that this had been easy to explain. On the night before the murder, Crichton had donned a clean pair of trousers and had then put on a clean vest the following morning.

At the conclusion of the interview Cameron asked Jean once more if she could recall having seen a vagrant in the area matching Betsy Riley's offered description. Her opinion was terse – 'Mr Cameron sir, that woman has been coming to my house for some eighteen years now, and I wouldna' trust her as far as I could throw her.'

Robert Barlas was also asked if he had witnessed any washing carried out on the day of the murder. The boy was fairly certain that he had seen Mrs Crichton working at the tub in front of her doorway, though could not recall which items she had been cleaning. This was at some point in the afternoon after he had had his dinner, and so he assumed it would have been past two o'clock. The conversation then turned to her husband – had Robert ever seen him smoking? The boy confirmed that he had – and within the ploughman's own house – though could not remember whether it had been before or after the murder. Neither could he recall anything about the pipe which he had been using, and was thus unable to say whether the pipe fragments were from that which he had used.

With the Barlas family re-examined, Cameron next travelled to each of the farms surrounding Mount Stewart, to question their inhabitants for any particular observations they may have made of Crichton.

Alexander McCathie, who resided at Glenearn in the adjacent parish of Dron, recalled meeting with Crichton on the day before the murder. The blacksmith remembered the occasion well, for he had attended Dron Kirk at two o'clock in the afternoon. It had been a fairly blustery sort of day weather-wise, though the rain had thankfully held off. He had set off from Pitkeathly Cotton houses and whilst walking along the road had met up with Crichton, who was travelling to the kirk for the same purpose. The ploughman had been dressed in dark greyish clothes, as he recalled, and had told the smith that he was travelling to the service without his master's permission. Henderson had forbidden him from leaving the farm to do so, but, ignoring him, Crichton had put his horses back in the stables at dinner time and had not bothered to return. McCathie had sat through the service with Crichton, and upon its completion both men had walked back along the road together, before parting ways again about half a mile from Mount Stewart.

John Sinclair, a shepherd in the employment of Lawrence Oliphant of Condie, stated that on the morning of the murder he had been looking after sheep on the farm of Dumbuils, which adjoined Mount Stewart at its western side. He had remained in the field until half past eleven, at which point he left to attend Condie House, about a mile away. The shepherd did not return to Dumbuils until later in the afternoon, perhaps as late as five o'clock in the evening. Prior to his departure from the big house, he had noticed Crichton some 200-300 yards away in the next field working with the plough. The man had been attired in ordinary working clothes, dirty moleskins or corduroys, which looked as if they had been worn for some time. Further pressed to state whether he may not have in fact been wearing clean clothes, the shepherd stated that he was quite sure this was not the case. Sinclair had not seen Crichton again for the remainder of the day.

Just north of Dumbuils, twenty-year-old Jessie McNeil had been working on Peter Robertson's farm at Baxterknowe. The steading was just a quarter of a mile away from Mount Stewart, though Henderson's property was blocked from its view by the small hill situated between the two properties. The servant had been putting the cattle out in the barnyard before midday, and had noticed Crichton at work with his horses some distance away on the Mount Stewart land. The ploughman had been facing away from her, turning his horses at the head-ridge of the field. He appeared to Jessie to have been finishing with his morning's work. When asked about his appearance, she too stated that he had been dressed in a jacket and trousers of a dirty, earthy colour. The items were most certainly not white.

At Southfield of Pitkeathly, thirty-five-year-old cattle dealer Archibald Harris remembered the day of the murder well, for he had been ill and therefore confined to his house while taking medicine. Between four and five o'clock in the afternoon, he had been forced to answer the call of nature. In making his way towards the privy on the edge of the yard, he had noticed Crichton ploughing the field immediately to the south of his farm, not a quarter of a mile away. He had remarked to his wife that the ploughman 'was going on the hill as white as a doo', meaning a pigeon, with his clothing appearing remarkably clean for a labourer at work in a muddy field with horses. Harris added that it was most unusual for a farm servant to change his clothes before the week had ended, unless the weather had been so terrible that they had become soaked with the rain, but this had not been the case.

To the east of Mount Stewart, the farm of East Dron was the next to be visited by the constable. John Richmond was the proprietor – he had not seen Crichton on the day at all, but noted that he had previously employed the ploughman as a cattleman in the year prior to his taking up employment with William Henderson. The farmer's grieve, John Robertson, was also interviewed, and recalled that during his time at East Dron he had observed Crichton take out a pipe on many occasions, and had often given him a light for it. He also took snuff from time to time, but the grieve could not say whether Crichton was still in the habit at the present time; he no longer had any dealings with him.

At the constabulary headquarters in Perth, Cameron's interview notes were mulled over by the constable, Superintendent McDonald and Sergeant Ross. It was now fairly obvious that Crichton had most certainly changed his clothes on the day. Was this the only untruth he had told them?

Despite the ploughman's recent assertions to Cameron that he did not smoke, it was also apparent that he had certainly been a smoker in recent times, but whether this had been the case just prior to the murder was still not clear. If it could be proved that the man was using a pipe at the time, the broken clay pipe and tin top found beneath the bolster pillow could prove to be a significant clue.

Seven fragments of the pipe had been found at the scene. Although some parts were still missing, the pipe's bowl was significantly amongst the pieces that had been retrieved. At its bottom the name 'G. and A. Kane, makers, Perth' could be easily discerned. Sergeant Ross was tasked with investigating who had produced the pipe and where such pipes had been sold in the vicinity.

The manufacturer was quickly established to be George Kane, a twenty-seven-year-old tobacconist who had started his business at 69 South Street in Perth at Martinmas in the previous year. The pipe maker was very easily able to identify the broken fragments in the sergeant's possession as belonging to one of a hundred gross or so of the instruments that he had made shortly after his arrival; he was absolutely certain of this, for the pipes were of a peculiar soft kind. They had been distributed to shops across the countryside shortly after and could be found for sale in the Bridge of Earn, Dunning, Auchterarder, Crieff and of course Perth itself; some had also been distributed in the town of Newburgh, in the north of neighbouring Fife. The manufacturer was unfortunately not able to provide a list of those to whom he had sold stock, for there were simply too many people in the district, including small merchants and hawkers.

The sergeant concluded his interview by asking Kane if there were any other deductions that could be made from the fragments presented before him. He lifted the bowl and the larger pieces of the stem and after a few moments of scrutiny stated that in his opinion the pipe had not been long in use, perhaps no longer than three or four days at most. It was therefore possible that it had in fact only been bought recently prior to the day of the murder. The sergeant thanked the tobacconist and before leaving his premises retrieved an unbroken example of such a pipe, to offer as potential evidence should the case ever get to trial.

Now that Ross had established the origin of the pipe, the next step was to try to establish where it had been purchased. It would be impossible to check every possible point of sale, but it could certainly be established from local stores around Forgandenny and the Bridge of Earn whether James Crichton had ever purchased such an implement, or whether he had been in the habit of buying tobacco.

The sergeant first made his way to the Bridge of Earn, where two shopkeepers were known to sell tobacco products. Accompanied by Constable Cumming, he first questioned forty-year-old James Deas, a partner with his father in the firm of James Deas and Company, the village's main grocery and spirits store. Being shown the fragments of the pipe, Deas was able to inform the sergeant that he had been dealing with George Kane ever since the pipe maker had first set up in business. He had bought many pipes similar to the one presented before him now, and usually directly from the manufacturer himself. When told that the pipe was a soft pipe, Deas replied that he could not tell the difference between a hard and a soft pipe, not being a smoker himself.

The sergeant asked the grocer whether he was acquainted with James Crichton, or if he had ever had any dealing with either the ploughman or any members of his family. Deas replied that he was certainly aware of the man, and confirmed that members of his family had occasionally visited his shop, but not frequently enough to have a pass book for credit. When asked what products were purchased from him, the grocer replied that it was usually Crichton's son who visited on Friday afternoons in order to obtain the latest copy of the *People's Journal*.

Ross then enquired whether tobacco had ever been sold from the shop to any member of the Crichton family. Deas could not remember selling any prior to the murder, but could confirm that about a week after the event James Crichton had visited the shop and had indeed bought some tobacco. The sergeant asked him whether he might have sold him a pipe also, but the grocer stated that he normally gave a pipe with any tobacco purchased, if more than an ounce was asked for – it was extremely likely therefore that he would have done so with Crichton. Might the ploughman have purchased some snuff also? To the best of the grocer's knowledge, he had not.

The sergeant and the constable retrieved another example of a new pipe from the grocer for evidential purposes, before exiting the building and making their way to Duncan Dewar's shop on Front Street. Dewar was a tailor and clothier by trade, but also managed a small groceries concern. The tailor's son, Robert, had kept the counter on the day of the murder, and stated that he could not recall Crichton having ever been present in the shop. He was likewise shown the broken pipe, but although he could not remember selling such an item to the ploughman, he was certain that he had sold him tobacco on at least two or three occasions. Asked how much tobacco Crichton would make in a purchase, the young lad apologised but could not recall, nor could he remember whether the purchases had taken place before or after the end of March.

The final shopkeeper to be questioned was twenty-eight-year-old Ann Wanton, the wife of Forgandenny-based joiner James Williamson. Her grocery shop was based in the couple's house at Carmichael Cottages, located on the main road into the village, about a quarter of a mile below the hill on which Mount Stewart stood. She recalled that at the time of the murder she had also been selling Kane's pipes, but that none had left her counter in the days leading up to the murder.

When the conversation turned to Crichton, Ann pointed out that the ploughman's family had only purchased the occasional loaf of bread from her. The first time she had ever met James Crichton was on the night of the murder itself when he had visited her shop in the late hours of the evening to obtain some candles. She had asked him at this point if he was 'the Linnlea man', to which he had replied that he was. The woman had then enquired as to the happenings going on at the farm that night, to which he had stated that he 'didna' ken, but it was an awfu' job'. The shopkeeper described how in the ensuing conversation the labourer had stated that he had observed somebody talking to Mrs Rogers at about eleven o'clock that morning. At this, the grocer had stated that it could not have been William Henderson, for she had seen him an hour earlier passing by on the road on his cart. She had also asked the ploughman if he had noticed whether the farm's kitchen door was open or closed when returning to his cottage at twelve o'clock for his dinner. He had not noticed. The sergeant finished his questioning by asking Ann if she had ever served William Henderson tobacco. Although the farmer was a frequent visitor, he had never purchased tobacco or snuff from her, and to her mind had never smoked.

The policemen left the shopkeeper and conveyed their findings back to Perth. Frustratingly for all involved, very little additional evidence had been found that could in any way point to Crichton's involvement in the crime. To all extents and purposes it seemed as if the trail was on the point of exhaustion.

As the term day of Whitsun approached in May, James Crichton finished his term of employment with William Henderson, and vacated the cottage at Linnlea. He found accommodation for his family at Glenfarg, within three miles of Mount Stewart Farm, but with so much suspicion attached to him he now found it considerably harder to secure employment in the local area. For a few weeks he was able to obtain a short stint of work with Barlas and Cairns, working for his former neighbour as a labourer, before the mason was forced to let him go. With the rumours of his involvement continuing to grow, Crichton could find no other person within the vicinity willing to take him on, and so was soon forced to return with his family to his native Fife.

Henderson, still firmly convinced that the ploughman had killed Janet, was glad to be rid of him at last. Like Crichton, however, he too was now finding it increasingly hard to live at Mount Stewart. On each visit into the kitchen he saw his sister's body lying before him with his mind's eye, just as he had first found it. Every night when he retired to sleep, the nightmares would also soon follow. It was becoming too much. Rather than take on another hand, the farmer let it be known to the estate factor that he did not wish to continue with his lease, but would remain at the house for a few more weeks until another prospective occupant could be found.

The tragedy of his mother's death had led William Henderson and his father to move to Mount Stewart. The tragedy of his sister's death would now see him depart.

TEN

THE HANGMAN'S NOOSE

In the early, darkened hours of Tuesday, 22 May, the citizens of Perth began to gather in front of the south wall of Perth County Prison. Many had set off from villages throughout the county to witness the rare sight of a hanging in the city. Others were travelling aboard a special train from Dundee which was due to reach the Fair City at a quarter to eight, with the execution scheduled for just fifteen minutes later. As daylight began to break, a crowd of almost 2,000 people had already assembled.

The appointed hour had at last arrived for Joseph Bell. There was no sense of jubilation. Whilst a handful of observers laughed and made merry, the majority had come to witness justice being served within their community in solemn mood. Many were angry at the sentence about to be carried out. Some disputed the need for a life for a life; others doubted the very security of the conviction itself, based as it had been on purely circumstantial evidence.

The crowd soon found itself hostage to the religious doomsayers, who exhorted mankind and the good folk of Perth to heed the lessons of the punishment about to be carried out before them. In the name of God they preached repentance, and having brow-beaten those listening to reflect on the despair of their lives, then sold them printed religious tracts bearing illustrations claiming to depict a true likeness of the condemned man. In marked contrast, the town's ministers had previously pleaded with their flocks to stay away from the event, whilst many employers had expressly forbidden their workers to attend on pain of dismissal. Despite the warnings, the crowds continued to gather.

It had been seventeen years since an execution had taken place in Perth; so long ago that the old, wooden timbers of the gallows belonging to the town had fallen into a terrible state, with some parts found to be decayed beyond repair or simply missing. As a consequence the authorities had requested the use of the scaffold from Aberdeen, which duly arrived on the previous Saturday. After pausing for the Sabbath, workmen had spent the early hours of the Monday morning erecting the large frame, which stood at some fifteen feet in height. In addition they constructed barricades in the adjoining streets to keep back the crowds expected to attend. A wooden fence was also constructed to surround the gallows, standing at a height of six foot, within which several county police constables were now standing on duty. Sets of roughened steps led up steeply to the place of execution and to a separate platform which had been constructed for members of the judiciary, who would also be in attendance.

Whilst the platform itself was visible to those watching, the area beneath was hidden from view by black drapes hanging from the top rail. In many ways these acted somewhat symbolically as a large ceremonial mortcloth, obscuring the black coffin under the drop which was awaiting the prisoner's remains once he had been certified as dead. Behind the large structure a hole had been hastily knocked through part of the wall between the prison and the old Court House in the early hours of the morning, into which a doorframe had then been hastily constructed. This was the entrance by which the condemned man's body would be removed for burial within the prison walls, away from the public gaze and as part of the sentence.

Inside the prison classroom silence engulfed the party of dignitaries from the legal establishments who had gathered for the occasion, now seated around a table anticipating the arrival of Joseph Bell. Amongst their number was Chief Constable Gordon. Although satisfied that justice was about to be done, the chief constable had been made aware that the prisoner was continuing to maintain his innocence. Equally troubling was the fact that a cloud of public uncertainty was growing over the whole sorry saga. It was for this reason that he had ordered a large body of the County Constabulary to attend the proceedings, to prevent any collapse in law and order should the public's tolerance of the events begin to deteriorate.

Throughout his imprisonment Bell had become quite popular as an inmate with the authorities, a few of whom were truly sorry that today would see him on his way to a higher jurisdiction. Just a few days before, the convicted poacher had agreed to have a *carte* taken by a local photographer, and in addition to copies being sent to his family, he had asked that each of the prison warders could be given a copy in gratitude for their kindness towards him.

A copy of the image had also been forwarded to Sheriff Barclay, who had himself formed a conversation of sorts with the condemned man. Having learned of his skills in the composition of poetry, Barclay had asked the poacher for a few lines, which the prisoner had been only too happy to oblige him with. Bell's poems had become something of a talking point in the prison. Most concerned his fate and were written within books and letters for friends and families. Virtually all maintained his innocence, as in a letter sent to an uncle based in Alloa:

Dear uncle, about the jury I must speak again;
But the words won't be the same,
For I have a clear conscience, which God can tell
Has your nephew, Joseph Bell.

Dear uncle, I cannot help speaking without amaze.
See how the Court did on the jury gaze
When the verdict of guilty did sound its knell
Upon your nephew, Joseph Bell.

Dear uncle, it is improper and unsuited.
Why didn't the jury do their duty?
But they didn't – and they know it well –
For they sold the life of Joseph Bell.

Gordon and Barclay were both aware of the sentiments within Bell's verses. The poacher had accepted his fate, and had indeed seemed quite cheery in his imprisonment, even joking with the prison chaplain over his final meal that he was eating his very own Last Supper. His demeanour had greatly impressed those involved with the case, including one juror who wrote to him in his cell, with comments reflecting his own difficulty in the part he had played in securing the conviction:

I can assure you that it is a very painful position to sit in judgement in a case involving life and death. As an individual I feel this the more, having for many years been opposed to death punishments for any crime. Had there been any way by which, with a clear conscience, a verdict could have been returned to prevent such a result, I would have embraced it. The rest of the jury, I am persuaded, would also have been glad to have done so.

As if to add insult to injury, the juror had continued:

> Your position is a painful one, but in some respects it is good. You were as
> much under sentence of death before the trial as you are now. The whole
> human family are under sentence of death. The difference in your case
> now is, you know the time this event is to happen.

Upon reading this letter out to the prisoner, the Governor had claimed these
were the words of an intelligent man. Bell had begged to differ. He maintained
that he would happily take the sentence of execution for his sins as a poacher,
but never for a murder for which he was entirely innocent.

Joseph Bell believed the press's involvement in his case to have been his
undoing. The prisoner had instructed his legal agent to send a petition to the
Home Secretary, Sir George Grey, to ask for his sentence to be commuted,
on the grounds that not only had the local jury been biased against him for
being English, but had also been influenced by the newspaper coverage of
the events leading to the trial, which he claimed had seriously prejudiced the
proceedings. Bell had further shared his thoughts on the press's role in his
case within a letter smuggled out of the prison by a cellmate upon his release
a week before:

> Those satiric and reproachable newspaper reports which came to him in
> the A.C. (Alloa County Prison) are too vague and groundless, and, if not
> huddled up through motives of selfishness, must have been got up from the
> pure want of something to fill up space (Bell hopes it was the latter). Those
> in connection with the press ought not to operate on any such principle as
> to feast upon the character of those whom they are so ignorant of.

The appeal had been rapidly rejected, with the Home Secretary stating that
he believed everything to have been in order. The news had been relayed to
the prisoner on the previous Saturday. His reply was that he had expected this
to happen, but it was observed by many that his spirit had fallen somewhat
following the ruling. Now, on the morning of his execution, it was with grim
acceptance that he had received the news that the same journalists were also
waiting for him in the prison classroom, ready to conclude their reportage of
the proceedings which Bell maintained they had helped to corrupt.

At seven thirty the entourage in the classroom was invited to stand for the
arrival of the condemned man. The sound of footsteps in an outside corridor
soon heralded the entrance into the room of the Reverend Mr Sinclair, the
prison chaplain, accompanied by one of the most feared men in Britain.

As Scotland had no executioner of its own, the sixty-six-year-old English hangman William Calcraft had been brought to Perth on Sunday evening to prepare for the event. Throughout the length and breadth of the United Kingdom of Great Britain and Ireland he enjoyed the reputation of being 'the finisher of the law'.

The prisoner now followed, escorted by two wardens. Bell's wrists were pinioned to the side of his body by Calcraft, who attached them to a leather body belt which had been previously strapped around his waist. In one hand the poacher tightly clutched a copy of the King James VI Bible, which had been given to him just moments ago by Sinclair. The condemned man was led to a seat between the chaplain and the Reverend Mr Milne of Perth's West Church parish, and instructed to sit down. A short service then commenced, with Sinclair reading from the 51st Psalm, entreating the prisoner to 'confess thy sin, if such it be, and peril not the chance of the loss of thy precious soul on the vain boast of an hour'. Bell's response was to simply stare at the minister with a fixed but calm gaze.

At the stroke of eight o'clock, the Lord Provost asked Bell if he had any last statement to make or if he had any last requests which could be granted, so long as it was within his power to do so. The poacher stood up and addressed the gathered dignitaries:

I swear by Almighty God, as I shall answer to God at the great Day of Judgement, that I shall tell the truth, the whole truth, and nothing but the truth. Gentlemen, I am as innocent of that murder as the child unborn. I do not know who committed the murder. I have no idea who did it. It was not me who did it. So for that reason I am, gentlemen, innocent as the child unborn.

With a continuing air of calmness, he then turned to thank the ministers who had shown him great kindness and attention throughout his incarceration, before finishing with 'I am going to die an innocent man'.

Sheriff Barclay approached Bell and shook him by the hand, assuring him that he would personally write to his parents to relay that their son had maintained his innocence until the end. Barclay ended by exhorting him one last time to confess, for the sake of his immortal soul. 'I want you to die in Jesus Christ,' he said, to which the prisoner replied, 'Thank you my Lord. I will. I die an innocent man, but I am quite prepared.' Taking a glass of wine offered to him by Calcraft to help numb his senses, he downed it in one, before listening as the Reverend Sinclair promised to send his final letters to his friends and family after his death.

The assembled party now formed an order of procession, led by the scarlet-clad Town Sergeants, the Lord Provost, the magistrates and two constables. The hangman then accompanied Bell, followed by the ministers and additional constables, including Gordon, with the members of the press bringing up the rear.

After a long walk through several darkened prison corridors, the procession made its way out to the scaffold. Bell paused momentarily at the foot of the steps leading up to the gibbet, his eyes drawn to the fast-moving clouds in the heavens above, before ascending unaided with what several newspapers would later describe as a 'jaunty air'. At the top he was guided to stand on the trapdoor by Calcraft, who then tied a leather strap around his ankles in order to prevent his straddling the drop when it opened. A white linen hood was placed over Bell's head followed by the noose, a simple hemp rope, which was placed around his neck and adjusted until the hangman was satisfied that it was securely positioned.

As a last gesture the executioner also shook Bell by the hand firmly, the warmth of his countryman's touch the last human contact that he would ever know. At this the crowd's mood began to darken, sensing that the end was now near. They started to hurl insults at Calcraft, whilst several women close to the scaffold began to weep and wail loudly. The hangman, ignoring the crowd's venom, approached the bolt securing the door and with a sharp motion pulled it back. The door immediately fell back against the platform with a loud crash, as the prisoner fell to his doom.

For four minutes the crowd remained silent, watching Bell's agonising death in full view. The drop being just a couple of feet, the prisoner's neck had not broken to cause instant death, as would be the case in years to come with the adoption of the long drop. Instead it was through a long and painful suffocation. The public watched Calcraft steady Bell's twitching body as it struggled against the rope. After an apparent eternity the spasmodic movements eventually ceased. Justice had been served.

For the next hour Bell's lifeless corpse remained hanging, until at nine o'clock the executioner loosened the ropes to release him. As Calcraft did so the rope suddenly snapped, and with the executioner unable to catch the poacher's body in time, it crashed to the ground beneath. This further infuriated those in the crowd who had remained behind, forcing them to again raise their voices in anger against him, calling him a callous bastard who would one day be hanged himself. Beneath the scaffold, a plaster cast was taken of Bell's head before his body was coffined and taken through the prison wall to be buried next to the grave of the last executed killer in Perthshire, John Kellocher.

The Blairingone Murderer was now dead. As the crowd began to slowly disperse, a lonely William Henderson continued to stand and watch, praying for the day when he could return once more to watch the killer of his beloved sister suffer the same fate.

ELEVEN

THE KEY

Four days after the hanging, Chief Constable Gordon was confined to his house with a severe cold; he would remain bedridden for the next fortnight. In his absence Superintendent McDonald deputised for him at constabulary headquarters, handling the usual day-to-day run of enquiries and occasionally visiting his ill superior at his home of Goodlyburn House for guidance.

A bill for the services of a constable employed to work at the new Crieff and Methven Junction railway was still unpaid, and McDonald was ordered to inform the company that its services would be withdrawn. Problems with vagrancy continued in the county, with concern raised in particular over a group of tinkers said to have now found their way to the Pitlochry area. Theft also continued to be a problem, but it was often impossible to identify the culprits. To McDonald's frustration, this did not stop the public from supplying a seemingly never-ending note of suspects. In a letter to Mr Williamson of Lawers concerning a recent robbery, the superintendent stated that there was not enough evidence to convict a gentleman of the name McKay, who was suspected by the recipient. The superintendent also explained that his father-in-law, a villain named Middlemas, could not have been responsible. He conceded that the man had indeed been a well-known thief in the area, but the simple fact that he had been dead for a considerable period of time effectively ruled him out.

Gordon soon recovered from his malady and returned to work. Throughout the remainder of June and much of July he found himself heavily involved with plans for the construction of two new police stations in Pitlochry and New Rattray. The need for better accommodation had been highlighted following a deterioration of the vagrancy situation in Pitlochry, with the arrest of some thirteen travellers, eight of them from Aberfeldy and Ballinluig.

To placate the complaints of a Mr Butler from Faskally, the chief constable wrote to Sergeant Collie in Pitlochry to keep an eye on the rest of the vagrants and to see what could be done within the law, but conceded that 'they seem incorrigible'.

The cattle plague continued to cause havoc, with a sudden increase in the number of infections affecting the county recorded at the start of June. The *Dundee Courier* of Tuesday, 12 June, recorded that some 6,615 diseased animals had now been recorded in Perthshire since the outbreak, with only 1,744 having recovered, the rest having either died of the disease or been slaughtered. Thankfully, as June and July progressed, the number of infections across the county began to dramatically decline. Despite the turn in fortune, prosecutions for the earlier flouting of animal movement orders continued to be made in the Sheriff Court, further tying up both the judiciary and the County Constabulary's resources alike.

More importantly for the stalled Mount Stewart investigation, various personnel changes were implemented within the force. The most significant concerned Sergeant Ross, who, having worked in the headquarters at Perth for over ten years, was now promoted to the well-deserved rank of inspector. Following the resignation of an Inspector MacGregor at Blairgowrie, Ross was redeployed to take up his post, despite the objections of Lord Kinnaird, who had preferred a candidate by the name of Stevenson. Gordon had responded to the objection by stating that he would certainly consider Stevenson for promotion at a future date, but that there was no better qualified individual at present than his trusted sergeant. With the adoption of his new position, Ross's involvement as a criminal officer within the investigation now came to a close.

Two constables within the force were promoted to become fully fledged criminal officers. George Mearns, the thirty-one-year-old constable who had spent a great deal of effort assisting the investigation in its earliest stages, was transferred from his post at New Rattray to the constabulary's Perth headquarters on 6 June. Joining him a month later on 7 July was another Aberdonian, twenty-nine-year-old Constable Robert Glass. A former carpet weaver, the fair-haired constable had joined the force in May 1864, but had endured a somewhat bumpy career as a policeman. Glass had initially been based in Dunblane, but an intended promotion had been cancelled in March 1865 following what had been perceived as an inappropriate address to the procurator fiscal of that town within the fiscal's own house. Now, just over a year later, it was apparent that he had sufficiently redeemed himself in the eyes of his superiors; he was appointed as a detective alongside Mearns.

By the middle of July, the new criminal investigation team was in place, with the two newly promoted detectives now working alongside John Cameron and under the continued direction of Superintendent McDonald.

———•———

It would not be until the middle of the summer that the next development in the murder investigation would happen, with the surprise discovery of one of the missing items from the farm.

On Saturday, 21 July, Constable Cumming set forth from his police station at Bridge of Earn to make his usual evening rounds, which took in the area around Mount Stewart Farm. As he walked past the two cottages at Linnlea he acknowledged the presence of the sons of James Barlas playing in the garden of their house in the sharp evening light, and then proceeded up the steep track towards the farm. Ahead of him he could see that William Henderson was in the yard, replacing a damaged wheel on his cart.

Hearing the policeman approach, the farmer set down his tools. 'Ah, Constable sir, the very man,' he said, as he stepped forward to greet the young officer.

'Good evening, Mr Henderson,' Cumming replied. 'How's all wi' ye?'

'I am fine Constable, thank you for asking. It'll no' be long now before I move out, as I have now found a buyer.'

'I'll be sorry to see you go sir,' replied the policeman. 'Everything fine here this evening?'

'Grand, Mr Cumming sir, fine as can be. In fact, I have been waiting for you to appear. Could you come with me into my kitchen for a few minutes? I have something I need to give you.'

Henderson led the surprised constable towards the kitchen door, which the officer noted was now bearing a new lock, and was invited inside. The farmer bid him take a seat, though Cumming politely declined, stating that he could only stay for a brief moment. William then stepped over to the fireplace, picked up an object from an iron hook, and handed it over.

'It's the key, constable. I've found the damned key.'

'The key, Mr Henderson?'

'Aye son,' said the farmer, with a slight frown of confusion, disappointed that the constable had yet to gauge its significance. 'To my kitchen door? You mind that when my sister's body was found that the door was locked? I couldna' find it for love nor money and had to get in through my window? Well, I've found it. That's it in your hand.'

The constable turned the large iron key around in his hands, which to his eyes appeared to have just been cast. 'How did you come across this Mr Henderson? I seem to recall we made quite a search for it around the premises, but with no success?'

'It was in the sink hole outside the door Mr Cumming. I was cleaning it this afternoon, and as I was lifting out the mud I found a couple of items settled in deep at the bottom. One of them was a fork – Lord only knows how long it was in there. The other was this damnable key. It must have been lying there ever since my sister was murdered.'

The young constable stepped towards the kitchen window and held the object up to the light to make a better examination of it, still puzzled by what he saw before him. 'Are you sure you have handed me the right key, Mr Henderson sir?'

'Aye lad, it has been sitting there all day waiting for you since I found it,' said the farmer, failing to note the young officer's confusion. 'Do you no' see what I am getting at Constable? There were only two people who ever used the thing – myself and that bloody ploughman of mine.'

'Yes, I mind you telling us that when we searched the place,' replied the officer.

'But there's the thing,' continued the farmer, having apparently worked out the obvious conclusion. 'I know for certain that it wasna' me that threw it in there. It *must* have been him.'

'The key does not look as if it has been in water for so long, Mr Henderson,' replied the officer, continuing to examine the object. 'I canna' see any rust or tarnish on it. I would have thought with it being in the pit for as long as you suggest that there must be at least some form of corrosion.' The constable lifted his handkerchief out of his pocket and rubbed it forcefully onto the base of the key for a few seconds; no sign of any tarnished residue was deposited on the cloth. He addressed the farmer once more.

'Did anybody see you make the discovery in the sink hole?'

'Do you doubt me son?' the farmer replied indignantly. 'I tell you this is the kitchen door key and that it was in that sink hole. My servant's wee lass was playing nearby, you can ask her if you like – she saw me clearing it out.'

'Thank you Mr Henderson, I will need to question her. What is her name?'

'It's Elizabeth; Elizabeth Bell. Her mother is Margaret Gibson. She's been with me for a few weeks now.'

'And where are the lass and her mother now?' enquired the constable.

'Both are away for the night, they'll no' be back until Monday morning,' replied William angrily, before composing himself once more in front of the young policeman. 'I'm trying to help you Constable, I thought you would wish to know.'

'And I am very grateful Mr Henderson. Thank you for this.' Sensing that the farmer was still somewhat irritated, he attempted to diffuse the situation further. 'Forgive me sir; I do not doubt your story. I am just astonished that the key should be in such good condition. I will be back in touch within the next few days – I will need to take this with me.'

'Very good Constable. I'll no' be going anywhere,' replied Henderson.

The constable thanked him and asked if he could be shown the spot where the key had been found. William led him out of the kitchen and to the small sink hole beside the door into the house. A pile of wet mud lay beside it, clearly the spoils excavated from the pool. The constable kicked part of it with his foot, and was surprised to see what appeared to be a small, metallic glint in the now orange evening light. He crouched down to investigate the cause of such a reflection, using his hands to further separate the soil, and was soon astonished to find that within the spoils there was in fact another key.

'This cesspool of yours has clearly developed a sudden propensity for producing keys, Mr Henderson,' suggested the constable somewhat ironically. 'Can you explain what this is used for?'

Henderson was clearly astonished. He brushed the mud from the item, which was similar in size and type to the object that he had already handed to the constable. Once it was cleaned he soon recognised it to be the key of the cottage at Linnlea, where Crichton had resided. When the ploughman had moved away at Whitsun, he explained, he had not returned the key to the farm himself, but had sent his son to do so. It had then been placed into his kitchen drawer. Why it was now outside in the soil he could only hazard a guess; perhaps the young lass Elizabeth had removed it and then dropped it whilst playing outside? Seeing no benefit in holding onto the second key, the somewhat bemused constable handed it to the farmer and bid him good evening.

———

On the morning of Monday, 23 July, Alexander Cumming conveyed the newly discovered key by train to Perth. After he informed Superintendent McDonald of Henderson's unusual story, a meeting was called with the fiscal, John Cameron and the force's two new criminal officers, Mearns and Glass.

The announcement of the key's discovery was met with a range of responses, ranging from complete surprise to utter derision. Holding the object in his hands, George Mearns stated that he personally had a great deal of trouble believing the farmer's story, for he himself had cleaned out the cesspool with a spade on the morning after the murder. When asked how thorough his examination had been, Mearns replied that he had absolutely reached the bottom of the hole, which was no more than a foot and a half deep. There had been nothing in the pit at all. If the farmer's story was true, and the key had been there, he suggested that it must have been disposed of at some stage after his examination. In lieu of the possible importance of the find, the new detective was advised by the fiscal to write up a precognition statement outlining his actions on that particular morning for submission to the Crown Office. In the meantime he instructed Cameron to travel out to the farm to question both William Henderson and his servant further.

Cameron made his way to the Bridge of Earn by train, accompanying Cumming on his return, before setting off for the farm on a hired gig. He arrived at Mount Stewart shortly after midday, and was greeted in the farmyard by William Henderson's new servant, Margaret Gibson. She led him into the farm's kitchen before going to inform her employer of the policeman's arrival. Henderson was feeding the pig and paused momentarily to cross over to the kitchen, where Cameron informed him that he had come to take statements from each of the farm's occupants about the key's discovery. He would start with his servant unless there were any objections – none were offered.

Invited to sit down at the kitchen table, Margaret Gibson was first asked to explain how long she had been working at Mount Stewart. The twenty-four-year-old servant replied that she had taken up employment with Henderson at the end of May, having moved to the property from Perth. She further informed the detective that she would only be working for the farmer for a few more weeks, now that he was selling up and moving away from the district. The criminal officer then asked her to describe the discovery of the key.

'I was engaged in milking the cows in the byre, sir,' she began. 'It was about half past twelve, and my little girl was playing in the yard. She came running into me at about that time to say that Mr Henderson had found a key and a fork in the gutter, meaning the cesspool sir. She wanted to know if I wished her to bring them in to me to have a look at them. I replied that she should, and so she returned a few moments later with them.'

'And how did the key appear to you?' enquired Cameron.

'Oh it was very dirty sir, and it indeed looked as if it had been in the pool. I told Elizabeth that we should clean it sir, and so we washed it in a bucket in the kitchen and then left it on the sill of the kitchen window to dry.'

'Presumably when you found it, Miss Gibson, the key must have been somewhat tarnished?' he suggested.

With a look of puzzlement, Margaret replied, 'Oh no sir, it was not at all rusty. Once I had washed it and left it to dry, I think it may have become a little reddish in colour then, but I did think that if it had been in the pit as long as Mr Henderson had said that it should have been much rustier.'

'What happened then, Miss Gibson?'

'Well, sir, Mr Henderson came into the kitchen and said to me that that great key has been got now, that there has been so much work about, and he then told me that the murderer must have dropped it into the hole.'

The constable pressed her to be more specific. 'Were those his exact words Miss Gibson?'

'Oh yes sir, he said to me that the murderer of his sister had dropped it in the hole, and then said that he hoped that the murderer himself might be so easily found. After cleaning it I hung it on a nail above the fire and I believe that a constable picked it up in the evening.'

Changing the line of questioning, the policeman asked her to explain her duties at Mount Stewart Farm.

'Well it's just general domestic work, sir – looking after the place, feeding the cows, tending to the fowl, and general household chores.'

'And has Mr Henderson been a good employer?' asked the constable.

'Aye sir. The murder of his sister has obviously been a great burden to him.' Margaret clasped her hands together, before looking up again. 'At times I have found it hard here myself sir, with so much attention with the press and such like, and it does sometimes alarm me to think that Mrs Rogers was murdered in this very room. But Mr Henderson has been very understanding.'

'I am glad to hear it Miss Gibson,' replied Cameron. 'Tell me, as a part of your duties, have you ever cleaned out the cesspool by the kitchen door yourself?'

'It was one of the first things that I did on the Friday after I started my engagement here, as these pools can produce a right smell in the heat. It looked as if it had not been cleaned in a long while. I have not touched it since then and I do not believe anybody else has done so, sir – until Mr Henderson cleaned it out on Saturday.'

'When you cleared it out, what state was the pool in?' asked the sergeant.

'It was very full, sir. I used a spade from the shed to lift out as much dirt as I could, and took it away in a barrow.'

The constable lifted the key from his coat pocket and handed it over to the servant, who confirmed that it was the same object that her daughter had brought to her. She was then asked to fetch Elizabeth.

Within minutes the nervous six-year-old girl was brought into the farm kitchen, having never spoken to a policeman before. Her mother led her towards the table, where the officer invited her to sit beside him. As she did so the detective smiled at her reassuringly, knowing that the young girl was most likely terrified of being asked to speak to a total stranger.

Cameron first introduced himself to her in a gentle tone to try to win her confidence, and then told her that he was very interested to hear about the key that Mr Henderson had found. He explained that one of his friends had actually tried to find it himself a few weeks past, but had been unable to do so – perhaps she had brought the farmer some good luck? Elizabeth giggled, her face beginning to glow with a mixture of both embarrassment and flattery.

'Now listen, young Elizabeth,' said the constable, becoming more matter of fact, 'I would be very grateful indeed if you could tell me what happened when Mr Henderson found his key. Could you do that for me?'

'Yes sir.'

'Thank you, Elizabeth. Now, when Mr Henderson was cleaning out the pool, did you watch him from the start?'

'No sir, I was in the kitchen, and heard him outside, so I went out to see what he was doing.'

'Did he call you to come out Elizabeth?'

'No sir, I heard a scraping noise outside and went out to see what he was doing.'

'Very good. And when you went outside, what did you see?'

'Well Mr Henderson had the key in his hands sir,' replied the young girl, at which point she suddenly frowned. 'He said something very naughty sir, and so I told him off.'

At this her mother, standing behind her, let out a small laugh. The detective smiled at Margaret and then turned back to the Elizabeth. 'What did he say that was so very naughty?'

Elizabeth looked to her mother, worried that she might be scolded, but Margaret explained to her that it was Mr Cameron's job to tell people off for being naughty, so it was fine to answer. Feeling reassured, she answered the question. 'He said "Lord Almighty I have gotten the key". I told him off, sir, for using the Lord's name in vain, as my mother has always told me never to do so.'

'And quite right young Elizabeth,' replied the detective, with a mischievous grin. 'I hope he said sorry to you!'

'He did not sir,' she replied indignantly.

Cameron feigned disgust before returning to his main line of questioning. 'What happened then?'

'He put the key down on the ground beside the pool sir, and then left it there. I picked it up and gave it a wash in the tub beside the door and then showed it to my mother. She was in the byre, sir.'

'And was the key very dirty, Elizabeth?'

'No' very dirty sir, but it was wet.'

The detective then lifted the object from the table before him and handed it to the girl. 'Is this the key that you found, Elizabeth?' he asked.

'Yes sir, I think it is.'

'Very well Elizabeth. Are you absolutely sure about everything that you have just said to me? Did you leave anything out?'

'No sir.'

'Thank you lass,' replied Cameron. 'You have been very helpful.'

The young girl smiled. Before finishing with her, the constable asked her if she could now identify the other key which had been found by Cumming in the spoils beside the cesspool. She told the officer that it was the key from the drawer, and confirmed that she had played with it after the farmer had hung the newly found kitchen door key up to dry by the fire. Elizabeth was then excused, as Cameron turned to her mother and thanked her for her time.

Cameron did not spend much longer at the farm, as Henderson had already outlined his side of the story to Constable Cumming. In the yard he briefly went through the main points with the farmer once more, assuring him that any possible conclusions that could be drawn from the discovery would be taken into consideration, before returning to Perth.

As with his colleague George Mearns, Cameron was highly dubious about the find. Margaret Gibson had claimed to have cleaned the pit herself upon taking up her current employment. The idea that she and Mearns had both failed to find the key prior to Henderson's discovery appeared to stretch credibility to the limit, and the discovery itself had the feeling of having been staged.

Two days later, on Wednesday, 25 July, Constable Cumming was sent back to the farm to retrieve the original lock, which had been removed from the kitchen door in order that a new mechanism could be put in its place. The farmer handed over what he claimed to be the original mechanism, and sure enough when tested, the discovered key was found to answer favourably. Although Henderson claimed that it was the original lock, there was no way to corroborate such a statement. The constable nevertheless took possession of it and returned it to Perth, along with the key.

It did not take long for the press to get wind of the development. In an article on Thursday, 26 July, the *Perthshire Advertiser* noted that the missing key had been found. It described how the cesspool had been 'cleaned and examined over and over again by both officials and non-officials' and concluded that 'it appears as if someone has thrown it into the cesspool very recently'. The discovery, it noted, was quite frankly 'suspicious'.

Henderson had raised the point that only Crichton and he had been able to access the key. Crichton was already a suspect; now questions were being raised about the farmer himself.

TWELVE

SILENCE IS BROKEN

On 5 September, the procurator fiscal received a letter from Andrew Murray, the Crown Agent who acted as senior legal advisor to both the Lord Advocate in Edinburgh and his deputy, the Solicitor General. In his communication Murray requested an update on the investigation's progress. A week later, McLean sent through a detailed report to the Crown Office, accompanied by a collection of precognition statements as given by various witnesses in the case to date.

In discussing why so much weight had been placed on Betsy Riley's evidence, the fiscal mentioned that at first her account had appeared to receive corroboration from statements given by Crichton and Robert Barlas, both of whom claimed to have seen someone walking past the farm in the afternoon. This had since turned out to be William Gormack, noted by McLean as a 'respectable old man', which had prompted the fiscal to seriously reconsider the reliability of Betsy Riley's testimony. Under the advice of Sheriff Barclay, he had then advised the county police to look more closely at Crichton's circumstances. Noting that although strong suspicions were attached to the ploughman, the fiscal explained that it was not thought advisable to apprehend him as the evidence gathered to date was still not likely to be enough to secure a conviction.

The fiscal drew his report to an end by first stating that, with the exception of the kitchen door key having been located at Mount Stewart Farm, there had been no further developments in the case. He then added that at every stage of the investigation he had drawn advice from the county sheriff, as well as his deputy, Sheriff Barclay. The police had been unremitting in their efforts, but had yet to find anything likely to lead to the perpetrator of the crime.

For the next few weeks the evidence was meticulously poured over in the nation's capital by the Crown Office, before being returned to the fiscal at the beginning of October. A note from the Lord Advocate followed on

17 October, summarising both his detailed consideration of the case and further proceedings to be taken in Perth.

The Lord Advocate first stated that he was under the impression from some of the statements given that the motive had been considered as plunder and robbery, and that the investigative team had concluded that the robbery must have preceded the murder. He observed that as there had been no marks of blood found in the pocket books within Henderson's chest of drawers in the bedroom, and from the quantity of blood in the kitchen, that it would seem more likely that any theft had in fact been committed first. It was therefore possible that Janet Rogers had been outside of the house before the arrival of the killer and had then returned back inside. In doing so she may have startled the perpetrator, a circumstance which might then have tragically led to her death.

To further support his theory, the Lord Advocate cited the evidence of the eggshells found at the scene. He noted that eggs had been removed from William Henderson's locked press, cooked and then eaten. This was clearly an act of great deliberation, and must have been done prior to the victim's death, for he did not think that the murderer would have hastened to do this after having brutally killed the woman.

When it came to Betsy Riley, the Lord Advocate disagreed with McLean's assessment of her reliability. He saw no reason to doubt the truth of her claims about seeing a witness at the door of the farm, even if the man had as yet to be found.

Attention was then turned to the kitchen door key, which had suddenly been discovered in July. Constable Mearns had searched for the key on the day after the murder in the exact spot where it had been subsequently found. Upon its discovery, the item was found to be barely tarnished, indicating that it must have lain there only for a short time. The conclusion that the Lord Advocate drew from this was that it was likely that the killer must have been a local resident – if he was not from an area close to the steading, why would he return to the place so many weeks later to ditch the key beside the very location where the murder had been committed?

The next item of evidence which needed to be considered was the broken pipe found under the bolster beside the victim's body. The pipe had clearly been manufactured in Perth, and items like it were found to have been sold in the Bridge of Earn and elsewhere within the neighbourhood. This was much more difficult to link to any suspect directly, but could still prove to be a useful clue.

The taxing question therefore centred on who the suspect or suspects really were at this stage. The Lord Advocate agreed that William Henderson could not have been involved; his well-witnessed presence in Perth and later at the Bridge of Earn clearly ruled him out. It was also clear that James Barlas was not suspected by anybody, and that even if he had been, he would undoubtedly have been able to supply as many alibis as Henderson.

James Crichton, he concurred, was a much different prospect. He had been within the immediate neighbourhood of the house for the whole day, and had known that his master would be absent in Perth until the evening. Crichton had been defined by some as sulky, vengeful and of a particularly cruel temper. He had also been on bad terms with his master, and there was still a strong suspicion that he had previously waylaid and attempted to assault him; notably intervening with the farmer's termination of Christina Miller's employment.

William Gormack's evidence was of particular interest in noting that Crichton had been unusually late in yoking his horses in the afternoon after having eaten his dinner. He should have returned to his plough shortly after his dinner break had concluded at two o'clock, but if Gormack's testimony was accurate, it was closer to half past three before he had done so. The work in which he had been previously engaged, the removal of the fence posts from the head-ridge of the field, should not have taken so long.

Then there was what the Lord Advocate noted as a 'very important fact', that according to several witnesses the ploughman had been dressed in dark-coloured moleskins on the morning, but had changed his apparel for lighter-coloured clothing by the evening. His wife had also been observed on the same day washing his trousers and vest. When questioned about his change of clothing, Crichton had appeared to have given false reasons for doing so. On the previous day he had alleged that it had been wet and that he had been soaked whilst travelling to the kirk; yet on that day there had been no noticeable fall of rain, it had merely been blustery.

The conclusion that would seem to best fit the circumstances was the fact that James Crichton was indeed the culprit, but, the Lord Advocate agreed, there was not yet sufficient evidence to warrant having the man charged. He therefore advised that the investigation should continue into the circumstances and character of both James Crichton and his wife. Everything that could be found out about them must now be done so. How this should be proceeded with, the Lord Advocate left entirely up to the procurator fiscal. The lines of investigation to pursue would emerge from consideration of both the precognitions taken so far and the police reports in Perth. It was suggested, however, that the 'investigations in this very important case have been hitherto left too much in the hands of the police' and that the fiscal should take a much more direct interest in the case.

The month of November would see further changes in the circumstances of many involved with the case. At the term day of Martinmas, thirty-nine-year-old Peter Stewart took over the responsibility of managing Mount Stewart Farm's seventy-five acres of land, moving into the farmhouse with his wife Grace. William Henderson had departed from the property a couple of weeks earlier and had now found accommodation at 135 Canal Crescent in Perth, renting rooms from a printer, James Robertson, who also resided within the building.

In another change, Constable John Cameron was formally appointed to be a parochial officer within Perth, relinquishing his responsibilities as a policeman within the County Constabulary. In his new role Cameron would now work to fulfil the obligations of the Poor Law, to assess applications for poor relief within Perth and to maintain a vigilant eye on those claiming such a benefit.

There was to be one more red herring in the investigation, when shortly after Martinmas the County Constabulary received word of yet another potential suspect. A thirty-two-year-old itinerant hawker by the name of James Boyce or Robinson had been arrested for a serious assault and remanded in Inverness Prison. Although Boyce was said to have been a native of Paisley it was believed that he was Irish in origin, and at times had claimed that he was a phrenologist, though his sanity was said to be under some doubt. As with so many other potential suspects, his appearance had been considered as a possible match for the man wanted by the Perthshire Constabulary for questioning about the Mount Stewart tragedy. When the Irishman had been asked to state his whereabouts at the end of March, he claimed to have stayed at John Hope's Lodging Houses in Callander. At this point the Inverness police had contacted their Perthshire counterparts.

George Gordon immediately wrote to Constable Preston at Callander with instructions to visit the premises and to make enquiries. He was to examine whether the suspect had indeed been at the lodging house, and if so to consider whether he had arrived by rail. He was also to ask whether the man had brought a small brown dog with him, and for any other particulars that the Hopes could remember. The suspect was to be transferred to Banff Prison within a couple of days, and so Preston was to make the enquiries urgently, dropping all other duties until his investigation was complete. The constable made the necessary enquiries but was soon able to establish that Boyce had indeed been within the vicinity at the time of the murder, and could not therefore have been involved with the events at Mount Stewart.

Throughout November the procurator fiscal, John McLean, became increasingly ill. For a few months he had been suffering from a pain in his abdomen and frequent chills, but with the rapid onset of jaundice it was now blatantly obvious to his physician, Dr Absolon, that the fifty-nine-year-old man was beginning to suffer from the unmistakeable signs of liver failure. McLean continued to work until 23 November, at which point the pain had become so intense that he was forced to step down from his position.

James Barty, a twenty-four-year-old procurator fiscal from Dunblane, and partner of the solicitors' firm Thomas and J.W. Barty, was asked to temporarily relocate to Perth to take over McLean's workload. Aware that the Mount Stewart investigation had now dragged on for some considerable time, the young solicitor reviewed the entire caseload from the beginning. On the basis of the points noted in the analysis of the case by the Lord Advocate, the new fiscal instructed the County Constabulary to once again interview several of the key witnesses.

The Lord Advocate had opted to give Betsy Riley the benefit of the doubt, and so the hawker was once again brought in for questioning before Barty. When asked how often she had visited Mount Stewart Farm the hawker stated that she was not usually in the habit of doing so, and had only met William Henderson on two occasions prior to the murder of his sister. On the day of the murder she had passed the place at about a quarter to twelve, but it was soon obvious that Riley was now beginning to qualify some of her earlier assertions. Questioned again about the stranger she had observed at the kitchen door, she admitted that she was not sure whether he was in fact a stranger or from the parish itself, as she could not get a good view of him. She further stated that she could not describe his facial features, nor could she remember if he had been dark or fair, though she recalled that he had been swarthy in complexion. The dog she had seen was not the farm dog – of that she was adamant, as she knew Henderson's dog quite well. Most shockingly, the hawker then added, 'I might be wrong for all that, as my sight is failing.'

It had been determined that Crichton's neighbour James Barlas could not have been a suspect, but he was also interviewed again, to see if further information could be gleaned about the ploughman. Recalling the events of the murder's discovery, he stated that he believed that James Crichton had grossly exaggerated the amount of time that had elapsed between Henderson's return from Perth and his seeking aid from the mason. It had all happened very quickly.

The questioning turned to any conversations that the mason might have had with the ploughman following the murder. Barlas mentioned that he had indeed had various discussions with him over the matter. On each occasion Crichton had firmly tried to plant the idea in his mind that the farmer had killed his own sister, though Barlas would not hear of it. Asked if Crichton had ever discussed the presence of Mrs Rogers at the farm, the mason replied that he had done so only once, stating that Henderson had spoken to him of her as 'that woman'. Barlas had never told the ploughman that Janet was Henderson's sister. Crichton believed that the farmer had deliberately concealed her identity in order to put him off his guard; his theory being that she might keep her brother accurately informed as to what he did during the days when he was not around. During his brief spell working as a labourer for Barlas after Whitsun, Crichton had discussed neither Mrs Rogers nor the murder any further. The last that the mason had heard, the ploughman had now managed to find a position of work at a farm called Brucefield, on the outskirts of Dunfermline.

Had Crichton ever been worse off for money? Barlas stated that this was not the case; in fact it was quite the reverse. He had never heard of him being in debt to anybody. His former neighbour was usually a silent man, but he did have a 'little hasty temper', though Barlas added that the ploughman was someone with whom he had never personally had any quarrel. He knew that Crichton and his employer had been on fairly poor terms, but this in itself was not unusual as the farmer was rarely on good terms with anyone. He also confirmed that the labourer smoked a pipe, albeit fairly infrequently, but could not say whether he had done so prior to Friday, 30 March, though he had certainly seen him do so in his house afterwards.

In going through the precognition statements that had previously been recorded, Barty noticed that there was one person who had not in fact been interviewed at all. Henderson's servant Christina Miller had left his employment well over a week before the tragedy, and it had therefore not been considered necessary to speak to her. Reading through the account given by James Crichton, however, the Dunblane man noted that she had in fact stayed with him for a few days just after the killing. If the ploughman had indeed been the murderer, what might she have heard whilst a guest in his house for almost a week in the immediate aftermath of the crime? Instructions were given to track down the woman at once and to bring her before Barty for questioning.

Little was the new fiscal aware just how important her testimony would turn out to be.

———·———

It took almost a week for Christina Miller to be located by the police. Following her employment at Mount Stewart Farm it was established that the young servant had spent a short period of time residing with her parents in Blackford before taking up a temporary post further north in the parish of Cargill. At Martinmas she had relocated again, this time to Tophead Farm, two miles from Moneydie village, where she had secured a six-month position working for farmer Robert Smith. With her current whereabouts identified, a constable took a written summons to her demanding her presence before the fiscal in Perth on 12 December.

Upon her arrival at the procurator fiscal's office she was brought before James Barty, with Superintendent Henry McDonald also in attendance.

The twenty-one-year-old woman was somewhat indignant at having been summonsed from her work, but appeared willing to co-operate in discussing her brief experience at Mount Stewart. The fiscal started the questioning by asking her to outline why she had left Henderson's employment in the first instance. She explained that during her time at Mount Stewart, the farmer had frequently tried each night to take liberties with her once she had retired to her bed in the kitchen. As a consequence she had been forced to stopper the door into the room with a spoon wedged between it and the floor. She had tried to fetch help from her agent in Perth, but the whole situation had deteriorated substantially when the farmer had locked her out of the farm late on the Wednesday prior to her dismissal. The two had subsequently had a furious row in the yard, at which point he had dismissed her.

'Mr Henderson claims that Crichton came to your assistance and threatened to hit him – is this correct?' asked Barty.

'I was only too grateful for Crichton's help,' replied the woman indignantly. 'If it hadna' been for him, Lord only knows what Henderson would have tried to do to me that morning.'

'He also claimed that you were getting too intimate with his ploughman – that you were undermining his authority with him?' suggested the fiscal.

'Och, the man was worried about me talking to anything in trews,' she answered with an air of defiance. 'I couldna' care less what he thinks.'

The fiscal next enquired of her movements following her dismissal. After leaving her trunk of clothing with Mrs Crichton at Linnlea, she described how she had travelled to her mother's house at Blackford, where she had remained until the Saturday morning after the murder. By then she had resolved to travel back to Mount Stewart to retrieve her clothes, and had made her way on the afternoon to the manse of Aberdalgie, about three miles from the farm, where she had stayed the night. It was from the maidservant, Janet Young, that she had first heard about the killing. On the Sunday morning she had then continued her journey across the fields towards Forgandenny, and had reached James Crichton's house by the late afternoon. The murder had of course come up in conversation.

'What did Crichton have to say?' asked the fiscal.

'By the way that people were speaking about the murder, he reckoned it had taken place between eleven o'clock on the Friday morning and two o'clock in the afternoon. He told me that he did not know who could have done such a thing, unless the woman's brother had carried out the act himself before leaving in the morning. He also told me that he had seen nobody about the place, and that when he had passed the building with the horse at dinner time the kitchen door had been shut as usual.'

'Did he say how long he had been away for his dinner?'

'No sir, we spoke little of it after that point. Some of my items of clothing were still at the farm, and as I was scared that Mr Henderson might have been the culprit I asked Crichton to come up to the farm with me whilst I retrieved them. He waited outside whilst I entered the kitchen to look for them. As I was leaving I saw Henderson, but he never spoke to me.'

'What happened then, Miss Miller?'

'Once I had taken my things I returned to Crichton's house. He and his wife allowed me to stay for a while – Martha's father and my father are related. I remained until the following Friday.'

Barty asked her if the topic of the murder had arisen during her stay there. Christina seemed unsure of how to proceed, and for the first time began to show signs of agitation.

'Crichton and his wife were both convinced that Henderson had killed her. I mind asking Crichton on the Sunday night at what time Henderson had come back from Perth on the Friday, and he told me that it was just after he had put his horses in the stable for the night.'

'Did he say how he had learned of the murder himself?'

'Barlas' son told him from next door. Henderson had fetched help from his father earlier in the evening after his return from Perth. Crichton kept saying that between the time of Henderson returning and then visiting Barlas, he had had plenty of time to commit the murder. He was right convinced of it.'

Barty then pushed to find out whether Miller had ever noticed Crichton smoking at Mount Stewart or throughout her subsequent stay at Linnlea. She stated that he had been a smoker before the murder, noting that a couple of days prior to her dismissal from the farm she had observed the labourer working at a bed of reeds, and watched as his pipe had fallen from his mouth. The shank had broken slightly but was still long enough for him to use for the purpose. The pipe, as she recalled, was coloured with use. Crichton had said that he preferred an old pipe, she stated, because it did not waste so much tobacco. When he smoked his pipe the ploughman used a tin top. The reason she was so familiar with the instrument was that at one stage she had suffered from toothache at the farm, and he had allowed her to have a smoke to try to soothe it. Asked if she could remember seeing any name on the bowl of the pipe she stated that she could not.

Before proceeding further, the fiscal asked Constable Mearns to pass over the new pipe manufactured by Kane that had been obtained as evidence by Sergeant Ross and Constable Cumming from James Deas in the Bridge of Earn. The fiscal asked her whether this resembled the one that Crichton had used prior to the murder. The servant replied that it did. He then asked her to take a look at the pipe fragments found inside the farm at the murder scene. She described the clay pieces as being very similar in appearance and colouring to those of the pipe smoked by Crichton. An examination of the tin top found at the farm under the bolster was also confirmed as matching that used by the labourer.

Barty then asked if Miller had observed Crichton smoking at Linnlea during the week after the atrocity? She stated that he had, but that his pipe had changed. His new pipe was only a day or two old in appearance, and it was fixed with a new tin top. This had not yet been discoloured with smoking and was most certainly a different item to that he had used when she had been at Mount Stewart. Had Crichton ever used snuff? She answered that he had; his daily snuff box was actually a horn with a cork plug, although he had a fancier box which he liked to use on Sundays.

Despite her attempts to appear calm, it was becoming clear that something was bothering the woman. She was refusing to make eye contact with the fiscal as she spoke, and her manner suggested that while she was willing to co-operate, she was not volunteering the whole truth. The fiscal leaned forward towards the servant.

'Miss Miller, I think there was more to your stay there than you are telling us.'

'Mr Barty, this is no' any of my business, sir,' she protested in alarm.

'We have an unsolved murder case here, woman, one of the most brutal killings in recent memory.' The young fiscal reached across the table and lifted up a sheet of paper. 'I have the post-mortem report here. It makes for fascinating reading. Would you like me to describe how they found the poor woman? Do you know what the killer did to her?'

'The Crichtons are good folk, sir . . . ' the servant interrupted.

The fiscal ignored her and started to quote from the document in front of him.

'Seven wounds were found on the upper part of the scalp, Miss Miller; one in the very centre of the head, five inches in length . . . An inch and a half to the left were another two . . . '

'Stop sir, please,' sobbed the distressed servant.

'The scalp was separated to a considerable extent from the skull. They found the woman's skull caved in, Miss Miller, with an axe. The woman fell to the floor. She died in the house on her own. There was no one to help her, no one to stop the villain who murdered her. Imagine if that killer had arrived just two weeks earlier, Miss Miller. Might you have fared better?'

The graphic description had clearly upset the servant. She lifted her hands up to her face, cupping them over to hide the realisation of horror over what had happened. As tears streamed from her eyes, the superintendent walked over and handed her a handkerchief. She wiped her face, and was allowed a few seconds to regain her composure, before McDonald addressed her.

'Lass, I think if you know something else, now might be the time to unburden yourself.'

Miller handed the handkerchief back to the policeman. A little nervously at first, she began to add to her previous testimony.

'I suspected Crichton might have been responsible sir. After I first went to serve with Henderson he had told me that his house had been broken into, and a watch and some money stolen. He also told me that he suspected Crichton for it, and that since the incident he never kept much money about the house. I knew the two did not like each other, and that they were on very bad terms. Crichton would often get his temper up when talking about the farmer, and often let slip about things he had done about Fife. Martha often cautioned him to hold his tongue when she was around.'

'Cautioned him about what, Miss Miller?' asked the fiscal.

'His fights sir,' the servant responded, with growing confidence. 'I think she was afraid that he might come out with something in front of me which might implicate him.'

'Crichton is quite a violent man?'

'Aye sir. He was forever getting into all sorts of trouble in Fife. He often stated that he wished something would happen to Henderson on the toun that would get him into a scrape. When I stayed with them he was very reluctant to speak about the murder, and only did so when I would start the matter. He wasna' the man I knew when I worked at Mount Stewart – no' as lively like. He seemed very dull and his spirit low. I had great suspicions that he might have been concerned with it.'

The servant faltered, but was again encouraged to continue by McDonald.

'There were two beds in Crichton's kitchen, I shared one of the beds with Martha, he and his boys shared the other. The children and I would go to bed first, but Crichton and his wife would stay up long afterwards, seated within the kitchen. This happened every night, and they would wait some time before starting to talk. I think they were waiting for us to go to sleep. And that's when I heard them sir.'

'What did you hear, Miss Miller?' asked the fiscal.

The servant began to sob once more. 'Oh those poor bairns, sir,' she cried. 'Martha would speak to me when alone during the day and she would tell me that it would be a good thing if it were found out who the killer had been. But I heard them sir. I've never told anybody what I heard until now. I wanted nothing to do with the matter, as I felt for the bairns, sir, who didna' do anything.'

Barty stood up and pressed her urgently. 'Miss Miller – what did you hear?'

Through tears of anguish the servant looked up at the fiscal. 'He killed Mrs Rogers, sir,' she blurted out. 'The bastard killed that poor woman.'

The room fell silent for a moment, as the shock claim was received by all in the room. The details then came pouring out. On several evenings Miller had heard

Crichton's wife tell her husband not to speak of the murder before the servant had retired to bed. Miller, however, was awake in her bed on most of the nights when they had started to talk. On one occasion she heard the ploughman say to his wife that if it was found out that he had killed William Henderson's sister, he would be as much of a doomed man as Joseph Bell, and would be surely hanged for it. On a separate evening, his wife had replied that if it was ever found out that her husband had killed the woman she did not know how she would get by, and that it would be a disgrace for their children. For seven months Miller had carried the knowledge of what she had heard, for she had 'felt for her fellow creatures'. It was a burden that she could no longer carry.

The servant's testimony was completed after an hour and a half of questioning. The fiscal told her that if her words were proved true, she would most certainly be rich as she would be entitled to claim the £100 reward. Miller was allowed to leave but was instructed to remain at her farm where the police could contact her further in due course.

———

Sheriff Barclay had been immediately informed about the servant's shock revelations. When asked for an assessment of the woman, the fiscal responded that although it was likely that her moral character was highly questionable, there was no doubt in the minds of those who had witnessed her talking that the evidence she had just outlined had been anything other than credible.

Two days later Miller was questioned again, this time in the kitchen at Tophead Farm. Her previous statement was read back to her by Barty, who then warned of the consequences which would be incurred if it was discovered that she had made any false statements. The servant was unflinching, adamant about what she had heard. Furthermore, having had a chance to reflect on the pipe fragments and the tin top that she had been shown, she was now under no doubts at all that these were remnants of the pipe previously used by Crichton prior to the murder.

Miller added that when she had left on the Saturday morning, she had asked to borrow five shillings from Martha Crichton. The ploughman's wife had only four shillings in the house, and so had borrowed a shilling to lend to the servant from her neighbour, Mrs Barlas. When the sum had been handed over to the young woman, Miller had noticed several pound notes tucked within the woman's bosom, though could not identify from which bank they had been issued.

Sheriff Barclay was now satisfied with the nature of her evidence – a credible witness appeared at long last to have been found. A warrant was drawn up immediately for the arrest of James Crichton.

THIRTEEN

HER MAJESTY'S PLEASURE

On Saturday, 15 December, James Crichton was apprehended in Dunfermline by Superintendent McDonald and John Cameron. Although Cameron was now working as a parochial board officer within Perth, the superintendent had requested that his former colleague assist with the arrest, he having played such a key part within the initial stages of the investigation.

The two gentlemen made their way to Dunfermline by train, and from the station then took a carriage about a mile to the south-east of the city to reach Brucefield Farm, where it had been confirmed that Crichton had taken up work at Martinmas. They arrived in the early evening to find the big Fife man working inside the stables with his son, who showed no sign of surprise at their approach. McDonald showed him the warrant and informed him that he was now under arrest on suspicion of having murdered Janet Rogers. The ploughman's only response was, 'Well a well'.

Arrangements had been made to convey Crichton to an inn close to the railway station. He was led inside the building to a private room, where Cameron then searched his clothing. One of his trouser pockets was found to contain a few coins, the other a small metal box with about an ounce of tobacco. The box was labelled and placed inside a small paper bag. McDonald and Cameron then led the labourer from the inn and towards the station, where all three caught the last North British Railway train back to Perth.

Half an hour into the journey, Cameron decided to have a smoke. When finished, Crichton asked him if he could use his pipe also. The somewhat surprised parochial officer allowed him to do so, but commented that he had not thought to offer the ploughman the use of his pipe as he believed that he did not smoke. Crichton's response was that he did so occasionally, at which point the former constable handed over the implement with a little tobacco.

The party arrived in Perth at 9.30 p.m., whereupon the prisoner was conveyed to the County Constabulary headquarters. His name, address, occupation, age and height were formally noted in the constabulary's arrest book, before he was taken next door and lodged within one of the City Police cells.

———•———

On Monday, 17 December, Crichton was brought before James Barty and Sheriff Barclay to make a declaration. He was cautioned that anything that he now stated would be used in evidence should the case go to trial.

The questioning began with the ploughman's movements on the day of Friday, 30 March. Crichton explained the instructions he had been given by Henderson in the morning, and described how he had witnessed the farmer and his sister talking in the yard outside of the farmhouse before his trip to Perth. He had ploughed the field beside Dumbuils Farm in the morning, before relocating at about half past eleven to the next field to the east, closer to the farm steading, where he had then continued to work until midday.

'What were you wearing on that morning, Mr Crichton?' asked Barty.

'A white moleskin jacket, a vest and corded trousers,' answered the labourer. 'I've heard what people have been saying, but those clothes were put on clean the day before.'

Crichton explained that his wife had been planning to do a wash on the Friday morning, as their eldest son David, a servant at Headmore Farm, had left some clothing for her to attend to. His own garments had become wet on the Thursday morning, and so he had changed into his darker Sunday attire in order to attend Dron Kirk in the afternoon for the Fast Day service. Later in the afternoon he had then changed into clean white clothes, and had worked in these in the corn yard until well into the evening.

Returning to his activities on the Friday, Crichton described how he had gone back to his work at about two o'clock in the afternoon, after his dinner. The first job he had attended to had been the removal of the large wooden posts from the head-ridge between the two fields. This he had accomplished with the use of a single horse and cart, taking between half an hour and an hour to complete the task. He had then fetched a second horse and continued with his ploughing work, continuing until the light had faded.

The ploughman then described how he had been putting the horses away when his master had returned. He was called to assist with the removal of a pig from his cart, whilst his master had put away his own horse and cart – something the labourer stated to be very unusual. Prior to returning to his cottage, Crichton had taken the barn door key back to the farmhouse, only to find the kitchen door locked; he had assumed that Henderson had locked it and taken the key, and so had said nothing to his master. He then outlined how within the next hour he had been made aware of the murder.

At this point the fiscal asked him directly about his movements at the farmhouse itself that day.

'Did you remove any money from the property, Mr Crichton?'

'No, I did not,' the ploughman replied calmly.

'Did you kill Mrs Rogers?' enquired Barty.

'I did not,' he answered, without hesitation.

The questioning turned to whether the ploughman smoked. He replied that he was not in the habit; he had never used a tobacco pipe.

'Miss Miller claims that you allowed her to use your pipe and some tobacco for a smoke to cure her toothache.'

'The woman is mistaken. I didna' have a pipe or tobacco to give her,' answered the labourer.

Questioned once more about his attire, Crichton refused to concede that he had changed his clothes on the Friday. The items he had worn on that day were the same as those worn on the previous day, following his return from church. He had put on a clean cotton shirt on the previous Sunday, but could not recall if he had changed the flannel shirt underneath at that stage. He had witnessed his wife washing his dirty clothes during his dinner break on the Friday. Throughout the rest of that afternoon he had kept his clothing clean, and had not changed his shirt again until the Sunday following the murder. Had the hare that he had caught on the Friday spilt any blood on his clothing, he was asked? It had not, was the reply.

Crichton was then directed to explain Christina Miller's presence in his house following the murder. He explained how, following her dismissal, Henderson had instructed him to remove her chest from the farm, and to take it to his cottage. Miller later came to pick up the trunk on the Sunday, and it was on this day that she had sold it to his wife. The servant stayed with them until the following Friday, sharing the same bed as his wife, while he slept in another with his sons.

After three hours of questioning the examination came to a close. Crichton was returned to his cell within the City Police Office. Both the sheriff and the fiscal had been deeply unimpressed with his testimony, particularly with his assertion that he did not smoke at the time of the murder, despite the evidence given by Miller and other witnesses. Barclay therefore had no hesitation in signing a warrant of commitment for further examination, authorising Crichton's transfer to the county prison.

Although severely ill at this stage, John McLean, still officially the procurator fiscal of Perth, was fit enough to go through all of the statements that had been gathered to date to see whether there was now enough evidence to bring a prosecution. To clarify certain points of testimony, several witnesses were again briefly questioned.

Amongst those re-examined was James Rogers, the victim's widower. The Airntully man had been specifically asked to recall how much money his wife may have had prior to setting off for Mount Stewart Farm. He replied that he had given his wife a £1 bank note, but could not state if she had taken any other money with her, though noted it would have been extremely likely that she might have had some silver in her purse. This £1 note had not been identified as missing before, and was duly added to the list of items that had been taken from the farm.

Janet McNab, the thirty-year-old daughter of Colin McNab of Monzie, had heard of the suspicions against Crichton and had also stepped forward to offer her testimony. She had previously worked for Henderson about a month prior to the murder, and stated that she had left after two or three weeks as the farmer had 'attempted to take liberties' with her. She had come to know Crichton fairly well, and described him as a quiet man. She frequently saw him smoking his pipe whilst there, though commented that he was always very careful with it. When asked to describe what the pipe might have looked like, she stated that she could not recall, except to say that she had observed him using both an old and a new pipe. She also noted that the ploughman had used a small tin top with his pipe when smoking.

Despite such new evidence, there was a blow to the investigation on Wednesday, 19 December. William Gormack, the old farmer who had walked past Mount Stewart at three o'clock in the afternoon on the day of the killing, passed away at his home at West Mill, his bronchitis and age finally getting the better of him. The old man's evidence had been cited as particularly important, for he had questioned the length of time that it had taken Crichton to complete his task in removing the posts from the head-ridge. Thankfully, the farmer's daughter could testify, at least to the statement made by her father, and to the fact that he had set out at three o'clock from his home, as she had been present.

The evidence was now stacking up against Crichton, and the fiscal was increasingly confident of success if the case was taken up for prosecution. On Saturday, 22 December, McLean formally petitioned the sheriff substitute for a warrant to detain the ploughman for trial on several charges. Barclay readily agreed, and authorised the further detention of Crichton at Perth County Prison until liberation in the due course of law.

At long last, somebody would now stand trial for the murder of Janet Rogers.

———

With the ploughman remanded until the return of the Spring Circuit Court to Perth in April 1867, the newspapers suddenly had something to report once more. The *Dundee Courier* had already noted on Wednesday, 19 December, that 'depositions emitted by Crichton are at variance with what he stated at the time the murder was committed', but now his further incarceration could be announced.

On Tuesday, 25 December, another important witness stepped forward to speak to the fiscal's office. Twenty-three-year-old farm servant John Fraser from Pitkeathly approached the police in Perth to state that he had actually been within the labourer's house at Linnlea just two days after the murder; he was quickly brought before James Barty at the procurator fiscal's office. Fraser first insisted that he was not in any way intimate with Crichton and had rarely had any conversation with him. On the Sunday in question, Fraser had intended to travel to Mount Stewart Farm, for having heard about the tragedy he had hoped, somewhat morbidly, to get a chance to see the body of the murdered woman. As it transpired, he never reached the farm, for whilst walking up the track towards the farm he had encountered Crichton standing in the garden outside his house at Linnlea. The ploughman's wife and children were at the kirk in Dron, but he had remained behind, and duly asked the young servant if he wished to come into the cottage to have a smoke. Both had then spent the next half an hour smoking, Fraser from his own new pipe and Crichton from one in his own possession.

At this revelation the servant was asked for any further details that he could remember about the pipe's description. Fraser noted it as being new, it most certainly having only been used for a day or so. There was no tin top in use that he could recall. As the two men had smoked, the keen young man had wished to find out more about the murder, clearly excited at such sensational news, and had asked a series of questions of the ploughman. Crichton had initially answered his enquiries, but it had soon become apparent that he had not wished to discuss the matter further and the subject was dropped.

On Saturday, 7 April, just over a week after the murder, Fraser recalled that he had been at work in one of the fields at Pitkeathly. He had observed Crichton ploughing about 600 yards away in a neighbouring field, but remembered it particularly well because he had observed the ploughman's wife attend to him on two separate occasions. It was very unusual to see a labourer's wife step out onto a field to visit her husband, or indeed any other servant at work on the fields, particularly twice in one day. On each occasion she had spent a considerable period with him in discussion, much longer on the second visit than the first, though he could not tell what the conversation had been about.

Barty asked if he had had any further encounters with Crichton since then. Indeed he had, answered Fraser, for the two had met again just a couple of weeks after the murder. At the start of the week in question both men had been ploughing within adjacent fields and so had inevitably met up briefly on a few occasions throughout the day. At one of these encounters, Fraser had asked Crichton for a light for his pipe. The ploughman had said that he could not help, for he did not smoke. The young servant had found this to be odd, having spent the morning with him just a couple of days after the murder doing just that, but had not pressed the matter any further. The two ploughmen had met on yet a further occasion just a few days later, with each working on adjacent fields. By now gossip had been circulating in the community that the ploughman had committed the crime, for William Henderson could not have had the time to commit such an atrocious deed. 'Time be buggered,' Crichton had responded indignantly, 'he had as much time to commit six murders.' This was the last occasion on which Fraser had encountered the ploughman.

———·—

It would not be until the second week of 1867 that the press could once again report on the case, with an extraordinary development concerning Christina Miller. The young woman had been interviewed further on Wednesday, 2 January, following her initial shock testimony. James Barty, worried that her nervousness might lead to her changing her evidence, had requested that Sheriff Barclay attend the questioning in order to impart the seriousness of the situation that the girl now found herself in. At this meeting she was asked to further describe Crichton's comments expressing a desire for something to happen to William Henderson. She had repeated the allegation, adding that the labourer had stated that 'he did not like to put to hands himself because it would be known if he did so, but that if there had been another man on the town he would have given him a thrashing many a time.'

She was also asked why she had sold her chest to Mrs Crichton. To this she had replied with surprise that she had done no such thing, she had merely allowed Martha to keep it in security for the money she had taken by way of a loan, although she had never returned to pick it up again. Miller had also been shown the broken pipe fragments once more, but now chose to be more careful with her words. She claimed that the fragments were from a similar pipe to the one Crichton had smoked when working in the reed bed, but that she could not swear it to be the exact same item. She had fancied that it was very like it, but that she believed the one he used may have had a smaller stalk.

With the questioning completed, Miller had been advised to return to her domestic duties at Tophead Farm, and had promised to do so. Over the next two days, however, it was soon discovered that she had in fact remained in Perth. She had been found in the company of a soldier by the name of Smeaton, a former lover with whom she had previously been acquainted. On the day of her examination before the sheriff, she had met the soldier on South Methven Street, and had afterwards shared a drink with him in one of the city's inns. The two were then discovered to have slept together in the city for the next two nights.

On the morning of Friday, 4 January, Miller had then made her way to Blackford to stay with her father, rather than return to Tophead Farm to resume her service. James Barty had by now been made aware of the servant's exploits in the city, and, more worryingly, to some of the conversations that she had been having with those keen to listen to her. The servant had apparently boasted that she was about to come into a vast sum of money, and with the soldier had even discussed emigration to America. When word of her behaviour reached the interim fiscal, he informed Sheriff Barclay, who, without hesitation, drew up a warrant for her apprehension. The document was hastily conveyed by train to Blackford on the following day by Constable Robert Glass, one of the criminal officers, who arrested the servant at her father's house and escorted her back to Perth. She was immediately brought before the sheriff, who demanded that she account for her movements.

Miller confirmed that she had remained within the city, but that she had done so for her safety. She had heard that certain people had learned of her testimony and were planning to travel to Tophead to try to silence her, though could give no names as to the alleged parties. When it was put to her that she had claimed she was intending to flee to America, she denied she had done so.

The sheriff simply did not believe her. Worried that without Christina Miller to testify the whole case against Crichton could collapse, he ordered that, unless she could pay a surety of £20, the servant was herself to be detained at the city prison until the trial of James Crichton.

Clearly £20 was beyond the means of a humble domestic servant. Christina Miller was herself now locked up in the very facility housing the man they hoped her testimony would help to convict.

FOURTEEN

TRIAL FOR MURDER

Over the course of the next three months the case was prepared for trial. In early February, a Perth-based solicitor called Henry Whyte was appointed as the law agent to defend James Crichton. With auctioneer and land agent Alexander Hay, the thirty-six-year-old solicitor had established the firm Hay and Whyte at 30 St John's Street, in an office facing St John's Kirk. As well as acting for the City of Glasgow Bank, Whyte was also the agent for the Chamber of Commerce in Perth. A murder trial was not his usual fare, but as with any client, his job was simply to pull together a defence team and to present the case to the court as effectively as possible. The solicitor immediately requested to see copies of his client's statements, but was frustrated to learn that the Crown Office had retained possession of them from the end of January and had as yet to examine them fully.

John McLean's illness continued to deteriorate considerably by the day, and it was soon no longer possible for the fifty-nine-year-old fiscal to play a part in the prosecution of the Mount Stewart murderer. On 8 February 1867, he passed away at his home on Rose Terrace. His obituary in the *Perthshire Courier* would note that throughout his career he had 'eminently enjoyed the confidence of the whole community, and from his courteous and affable personal demeanour he was highly esteemed by all – rich and poor.' In due course his position would be taken over by fifty-three-year-old Cupar-born solicitor Melville Jameson, but in the interim his much younger counterpart, James Barty, would continue to act with zeal over the case from his office in Dunblane. On Tuesday, 22 January, Barty had again posted copies of all the precognition statements taken in Perth to the Crown Agent, with an accompanying letter outlining the latest developments with Christina Miller. In this he had stated that he still had no doubts as to the truth of the servant's evidence, but added, 'On the other hand, there is no doubt that her moral character is bad.'

The Crown Agent replied to his letter, requesting actions on several fronts. He first wished to learn in what way had the woman been considered to have a bad moral character – had she been convicted of any crime in the past? He also wished to clarify that the servant girl had not in any way had a chance to be at Mount Stewart Farm at the time of the murder.

With regard to the second point, Miller was questioned again on Monday, 18 February, and maintained that she had been at Blackford before the murder and at Aberdalgie Manse on the Saturday after. The maid from the manse at that time, Janet Young, was summonsed for interview also, but she revealed her belief that the servant had been at the big house on the Saturday before the murder, rather than after. Miller was brought before the maid in the fiscal's office, but upon hearing the young woman's testimony the prisoner merely replied that she could not explain why Young was saying such a thing – she must simply be mistaken.

In a letter dated Tuesday, 19 March, Barty suggested to the Crown Office that it should seriously reconsider dropping the testimony of Betsy Riley, having omitted her from the prospective list of witnesses. The fiscal felt that to do so would be dangerous for a couple of reasons. In the first instance, he suggested, the defence would almost certainly try to maintain that the person guilty of the murder was William Henderson. The hawker's evidence would help to counter that effectively, for she had been at the farm at midday and could add to the evidence that the farmer was not on the premises. While it was not the most convincing of arguments, the second reason certainly bore more weight. If Crichton's solicitor noted the omission of Riley as a witness, he could easily allege that the prosecution had been afraid to put her on the witness stand because it was aware that her evidence was deeply flawed. The prosecution would do well not to undermine a witness that had been so extensively written about by the press. The point was conceded.

The name of the pipe maker, George Kane, was also added to the list, as he could testify to the fact that the type of pipe found at the scene was only available within the district surrounding the farm. Barty also suggested removing Elizabeth Bell and Margaret Gibson, stating that they could only speak to the finding of the kitchen door key in the extraordinary circumstances as had happened. He further added, 'There is very little doubt that Henderson put the key into the cesspool with the view of throwing suspicion on Crichton'. On this he was overruled; their names remained on the list.

On 30 March 1867, the indictment was completed and served on Crichton within the county prison, with Constable Glass there to witness the charge, which was clear and to the point.

You, the said James Crichton did, wickedly and feloniously, attack and assault Janet Henderson or Rogers, now deceased, wife of James Rogers, labourer, now or lately residing at or near Airntully, in the parish of Kinclaven, and shire aforesaid, and did with an axe, or other instrument to the prosecutor unknown, strike her several or one or more severe blows on or near the head, whereby her skull was fractured; by all which, or part thereof, the said Janet Henderson or Rogers was mortally injured, and in consequence thereof immediately or soon thereafter died, and was thus murdered by you the said James Crichton.

It would now be up to a jury to prove his guilt or innocence.

—————

The Circuit Court of Justiciary returned to Perth in April 1867 for its spring sitting. Sir George Deas, Lord Deas, was the presiding judge for the occasion, ably assisted by Lord Justice-Clerk Patton, with both men arriving in the city on the first Saturday of the month to take up temporary residence at the Royal George Hotel. As per tradition, on Monday, 8 April, the judges went through the usual ceremony of travelling to the court by carriage, escorted by a troop of the 4th Hussars, and accompanied by many of the legal establishment. Sheriff John Tait, who had by now replaced Edward Strathearn Gordon as the county sheriff for Perthshire, and his deputy, Sheriff Substitute Barclay, both attended, along with several local magistrates and other dignitaries. Among the local country gentlemen Lord Kinnaird was also present, as were Sir Patrick Thriepland, John Graham Murray and the Earl of Mansfield. The band of the Perthshire Rifle Volunteers led the procession.

On this occasion the Circuit Court would sit for the first time in a recently completed, and purpose-built, courthouse. Within the magnificent structure the new courtroom was laid out in a similar manner to that at nearby Dundee, though was believed to be larger by the reporters in attendance. The press was particularly delighted to note that accommodation for the profession had been substantially improved from the previous cramped arrangements.

For the first day of proceedings, the usual mix of cases was heard. A murder trial involving a lunatic was dismissed before it was even heard; two poachers were sentenced to seven years of penal servitude for assault; and a woman was freed when the evidence against her alleged concealment of a pregnancy could not be substantiated. With the first day's sitting ended, these were not the cases discussed by the citizens of Perth. Beside the large open fires in the city's inns and hotels, on the gas-lit cobbled pavements of its ancient wynds and vennels, and within the comfortable security of the cottages and tenements in the city centre and beyond, the main conversation was the forthcoming trial of James Crichton.

On Tuesday, 9 April 1867, the Mount Stewart Murder trial finally got underway. Quite unlike the previous day's hearings, the new Court House was crowded long before the arrival of their Lordships, with those desperate to witness the event clambering to find room amongst the packed wooden benches. Large numbers who had failed to gain admittance waited outside in the hope of gleaning any particulars from those coming and going from the building.

At ten o'clock, James Crichton was escorted into the courtroom by two constables of the county force and led to the dock. Dressed in a black suit of clothes, the prisoner was noted by the *Dundee Courier and Argus* as having features indicative of a man 'possessing great firmness and nerve'. The paper noted in particular that his bushy beard had rather improved his appearance; the prison authorities had evidently 'bestowed unusual pains in attending to his toilette'. It was also observed that his imprisonment had not seemed to act prejudicially against him, for he was 'as stout and healthy looking as he had been on the day on which he was apprehended'.

As soon as the ploughman was seated he was approached by his counsel, a solicitor named Charles Scott, who, under the guidance of Henry Whyte and the rest of the now seated defence team, would be acting for him on the floor. Scott reassured him that his defence was prepared and that he should remain calm throughout the day's events. The labourer listened intently whilst looking around him to see who else was present in the room.

The room was brought to order and the full indictment then read out. The charges were detailed against the labourer, followed by a list of the evidence that would be presented and the names of the witnesses to be called. With the statement completed, Lord Deas asked Crichton whether he wished to plead guilty or not guilty to the charge. There was no hesitation.

'Not guilty, my Lord.'

With the plea entered, the jury was then empanelled. As was common for Scottish criminal cases, there were fifteen jurors, each of them male, aged between twenty-one and sixty, and holding the relevant property qualifications. Six of them were farmers with considerable holdings across

Fifeshire and Perthshire; five were skilled craftsmen, with the remainder drawn from the merchant classes. The public observed as they took the oath: 'You swear by God, and as you shall answer to God at the great Day of Judgement, that you shall well and truly try, as the case may be, this issue, and a true verdict give according to the evidence.' With the procedure soon completed, the jurors would now listen to the proceedings before retiring to consider the evidence.

There were three possible verdicts that could be arrived at under the Scottish criminal system. If Crichton was found to have committed the murder, he would be 'guilty', and the hangman's noose would be his reward. If the ploughman was found to be innocent of the charge, he would be found 'not guilty' and allowed to walk free. The third possible verdict was that recognised in Scots Law as 'not proven'. To many this was an unhappy outcome, a verdict once described by Sheriff Barclay as that 'which at once gives a door of escape to a timid and vacillating jury, and leaves a stain on the character of the accused'. Not proven suggested that a suspect might be guilty, but that the level of proof was not sufficient to convict or condemn. It would also see the accused acquitted.

Sheriff Barclay was called briefly to testify that the prisoner's declaration, recorded on 17 December, had been made by Crichton when in a sound and sober state, and after the due caution had been correctly given. He confirmed that the procedure had been entirely regular. The Crown's case for the prosecution could now commence.

William Henderson was the first witness to be called by the prosecution. James Adam, the Advocate Depute, asked the farmer to recall the relevant circumstances at Mount Stewart, both prior to the events of Friday, 30 March 1866, and on the day itself. The farmer explained that he had recently sacked Christina Miller, his servant, and that his sister had come to help in her place, having made the journey to the farm on the Wednesday. On the Friday morning the two had breakfasted together, before he had left for the market at Perth. He outlined his trip to the city, and then his eventual return, explaining that he had reached the Bridge of Earn shortly after six o'clock, and his farm just after seven.

Despite the emotional difficulty of having to do so publicly, Henderson then outlined the sequence of events that had led him to the discovery of his sister's body in the farmhouse. He explained how he had put his horse away, before finding the kitchen door to be locked, forcing him to gain access via an upstairs window. The farmer described his efforts to fetch help and detailed the chronology of the police's arrival, and that of the procurator fiscal and the two doctors.

During questioning about the state in which he had found his overturned bedroom, Henderson mentioned that he had been surprised that his old silver watch had not been taken. Indeed, the same watch had been left when the house had been broken into some months earlier. Lord Deas intervened to ask if the watch had been worthless. 'It was not first class,' the farmer had responded, unintentionally drawing laughter from the public benches.

Henderson then described a conversation he had previously had after first hiring Crichton at Martinmas 1865. The ploughman had been informed that many fires had broken out at farms due to the negligence of parties smoking, and that he was therefore not to smoke about the steading. Crichton had reassured his new master that he would not do so. Finishing his examination of the witness, Mr Adam asked the farmer to briefly describe the unusual circumstances by which the kitchen door key had allegedly been found, before retiring from the floor with no further questions for the witness.

Henderson was then cross-examined by Mr Scott, who asked him to discuss the relationship he had endured with his female servants. He responded that he had engaged a few servants at various times, and that between servants, Crichton's wife had occasionally helped out at the farm. Scott pushed him to discuss why he had not let Christina Miller in on the Wednesday night upon her return from Perth. The farmer responded that he did not know that it was her, having assumed that she had stayed in Perth.

The farmer was then asked to explain why he had previously dismissed Christina Miller from his service. Henderson replied that it was because of the woman's insolence, and denied that he had ever tried to bed her – despite the fact that she had often claimed that the farmer would be better with a wife, and that she might be that mistress. He explained that he had soon grown tired of her discussions on the matter, at which point her attentions had then turned towards the ploughman, who would quickly come to her defence in any subsequent argument between the master and his servant.

'If I said a word to her, the prisoner would get up in a rage at me,' the farmer added. 'He often followed me to strike me.'

James Rogers was the next person to be called to the stand by Mr Adam. The nervous labourer was somewhat distressed, but described how he had given Janet a £1 note before she had left Airntully, and that she had intended to stay with her brother until he could find a trustworthy servant. Rogers was then questioned about his encounters with Crichton on the Sunday after the murder, to which he recounted the conversation with the prisoner in which the ploughman had accused Henderson of having killed his sister before setting off for Perth. Rogers had shown him how that could not have been possible, for he had claimed to have seen Janet talking to a stranger at about eleven that morning, and yet it had been proven that Henderson had left an hour earlier. The victim's daughter, Ann, was also questioned, and confirmed that her mother had taken snuff for a sore nostril complaint, but that she had never smoked. Ann revealed that when her mother had left Airntully she had also been wearing a small ring, but neither she nor her father had seen the ring since.

James Barlas was asked to recall the evening of the murder, and his small part in advising the farmer to fetch the police and Dr Laing from the Bridge of Earn. He described how Henderson had been a little agitated after finding his sister's body, but that there had been nothing else noticeable about his reaction. The Advocate Depute asked him to confirm that he had seen Crichton smoking on several occasions during his service at Mount Stewart, to which he replied that he had. Indeed, he had also done so when working for the mason himself. The witness was then handed to Mr Scott for cross-examination. Had Crichton ever smoked during working hours? Barlas replied that he had not.

The court then turned to the medical evidence concerning the attack on Janet Rogers. Dr Laing of the Bridge of Earn was invited to share his testimony of the night in question. He confirmed that upon being summonsed by Henderson, he had made his way with the farmer towards Mount Stewart immediately. The physician described the appalling condition in which he had found the victim's body, and was then invited to read out the full report of the post-mortem carried out by himself and Dr Absolon. As the gruesome findings were relayed to the court there were audible gasps within the chamber, as the true ferocity of the victim's injuries were outlined. Upon completing the account, Mr Adam asked the physician to clarify the conclusions that he had drawn from the post-mortem.

'Would death have been instantaneous after such an attack, Doctor?'

'Most certainly,' replied Laing.

Pressed by Lord Deas to confirm his estimate over the time of death, the physician stated that he did not believe it could have been any later than three o'clock in the afternoon. Whoever had killed Janet Rogers could certainly have not done so without getting blood on his clothing. He further noted that when examining the clothes of both the defendant and William Henderson, he had been surprised at just how clean Crichton's clothes had been.

A member of the jury asked whether there had been any food discovered within the victim's stomach. There had, but the doctor could not say whether it had been the remains of the victim's dinner or from an earlier meal. Lord Deas interjected again.

'That is a very pertinent question. Did you not think, Doctor, to take particular notice of that?'

'No, my Lord. We witnessed a bulky mass in the process of digestion, but when we found that the wounds were sufficient to cause death, we did not examine her remains any further.'

'Can you form any opinion as to whether the process of digestion was long or newly begun?' asked Lord Deas.

'I am afraid not, my Lord. As I have stated, neither Dr Absolon nor myself paid any attention to that.'

It was soon time for the police to be interrogated over its handling of the investigation into the murder. Superintendent McDonald was asked to discuss the evidence that was secured at the scene of the crime, including the pipe fragments and the tin lid found under the bolster by the fire. He stated that although Crichton had given no ground for suspicion on the night of the murder itself, the policeman had certainly believed that he had had a good opportunity to commit the deed.

McDonald then described the arrest of the ploughman near Dunfermline in the middle of December, and noted that Cameron had offered him a smoke in the train carriage. A somewhat surprised Lord Deas asked him, 'Do the police now smoke in railway carriages Mr McDonald?' drawing further laughter from the public, before his Lordship was advised that Cameron was at that stage working as a parochial officer.

Chief Constable Gordon and Constable Alexander Cumming then corroborated McDonald's findings. The young constable also deponed that although he had taken possession of the kitchen door key on 21 July, and the lock a few days later, the lock had not been removed from the door in his presence.

Jean Barlas was asked to take the stand, to confirm that she had observed Mrs Crichton washing clothes on the day of the murder. She added that, on the following day, she had observed a vest, trousers and a jacket bleaching on the grass outside the cottage, where they remained until the Monday. Responding to a juror's enquiry about Crichton's dress on the Fast Day of Thursday, 29 March, the mason's wife stated that the clothes he had been wearing on that day were grey in colour, and were certainly not white moleskins.

It would not be until one o'clock that the key witness of the case would finally be called to the stand. As Christina Miller took her seat, members of the press strained forward on their seats to see for themselves the woman who had finally precipitated the trial after so many months of maintaining her silence. Having been imprisoned for almost three months, the young servant's spirits had clearly been heavily dampened by her ordeal. She was nevertheless in perfect health, and attired in a new grey dress that had been supplied to her in prison by her mother. As the sound of the public's curiosity filled the chamber, Lord Deas called the courtroom to order.

With the short term of her stay at Mount Stewart established, the Crown moved quickly to interrogate the servant on the most important part of her evidence. Under examination by both the Advocate Depute and the judge, Miller repeated how she had come to stay at the ploughman's cottage for just under a week in the aftermath of the murder. During her residence there, she described how she had heard both James Crichton and his wife discussing the murder long after she had gone to her bed.

'How long had you been in bed before you heard them talking about the murder, Miss Miller?' asked Mr Adam.

'I could not exactly say,' she replied humbly, clearly not enjoying the public gaze.

'What did you hear Crichton say?'

'He said that if it was found out that he had committed the murder, he would be hanged for it.'

At this revelation the chamber erupted in outrage, before the public was silenced once more by Lord Deas. Miller continued, adding that the ploughman's wife had responded that the family would be disgraced if it should ever be discovered.

The Advocate Depute then asked the servant to confirm whether she had ever seen Crichton smoking. She had, came the reply, and on many occasions. With this, the Crown's representative stated that he had no further questions. He returned to his seat as the impact of Miller's testimony resounded throughout the chamber.

Charles Scott rose slowly to challenge the witness on behalf of the defence. To undermine her sensational allegations, a very different line of attack would need to be pursued. Ignoring the servant's testimony about her stay at Linnlea, he instead asked the young woman to cast her mind back to her final days of employment at the farm. Why had she travelled into Perth on the Wednesday before she was dismissed? Miller responded that she had wanted to get more peace at her work.

'More peace, Miss Miller? You mean you went to ask for another position?'

'No sir, I went to get more peace.'

'I cannot understand that Miss Miller,' said the solicitor, feigning disbelief. 'Did you consult with anybody whilst in Perth?'

'I went to see Mrs Lockersie, the register keeper, to ask for her assistance.'

'And at what time did you return to Mount Stewart Farm?'

'It was dark. I must have reached the farm at about ten o'clock.'

'And did you meet anybody on the road, Miss Miller?'

'Aye sir, I met a man as I was turning to come out of the Edinburgh Road.'

'And who was that?' enquired the solicitor.

'It was an Irish child sir,' replied the servant. The chamber erupted into fits of laughter.

'An "Irish child", Miss Miller? Did you and this "Irish child" go to Mount Stewart?'

'Yes sir,' answered the servant, her face slowly reddening under the full public glare.

'And what did you and he do there?'

'He just accompanied me, sir.'

'But what did you and he do when you got back to Mount Stewart farmhouse?' pushed the solicitor.

'He just stopped back, sir. I went to the house, but the door was locked.'

'And I am sure that must have been of major inconvenience, Miss Miller. I assume you called for Mr Henderson to come and open the door?'

'I did sir, but he wouldna' answer.'

'Where did you and your young companion then go, Miss Miller?'

'Because I could not get in I went and slept in the byre till morning.'

'And the man, too?'

'Aye, sir,' replied the witness sheepishly, as the crowd once more burst into laughter.

Lord Deas silenced the room and asked the servant if the man had also slept there, to which Miller replied no – he had stood by the door initially, before seating himself on a trough. Scott then continued with his line of attack.

'When did this "Irish child" leave the farm, Miss Miller?'

'I could not rightly say, sir.'

'Have you no guess? Would it have been about six o'clock in the morning?'

'I could not say sir,' the servant replied, now aware from the continuous laughter in the chamber that she was being openly humiliated in front of the general public.

Scott knew that the woman's character was rapidly falling apart before the court's eyes, and pushed forth his attack.

'What was the name of this gentleman friend, Miss Miller?' asked the solicitor, again to the crowd's amusement.

'I canna' say sir. I canna' mind it.'

'You have forgotten it, Miss Miller? Three weeks ago, I believe that you stated under questioning that his name was Higgin.'

'Aye sir. That was his name,' replied the embarrassed servant.

The solicitor then asked Miller why she had left William Henderson's service on the following day.

'Because I could not get my meat and he was always coming to me when I was in my bed,' she answered, her indignation once again finding a voice, but clearly at odds with Henderson's own testimony on the matter earlier in the day. The chamber erupted once more, the crowd clearly enjoying what was turning into an assassination of the woman's moral character.

Redirecting the witness to the circumstances of her apprehension, Scott then asked about her movements following her initial release after questioning.

'Did you meet a soldier called John Smeaton when you were in Perth, Miss Miller?'

'Aye sir, we are old friends.'

'Indeed, Miss Miller,' noted the solicitor with apparent disdain. 'And you stayed with him in the city for two nights?'

'Yes, sir.'

'I am presuming that he did not stand in by the doorway?' prompted Scott sardonically. 'You slept together?'

'You already ken that we did,' was the haughty response from the now heavily affronted woman.

'And did you tell Smeaton anything about the investigation?'

'I told him what had been said to me in the fiscal's office – that if my words were proved correct I would be rich.'

As the public roared again, the solicitor turned to them with raised eyebrows and a dismissive look of amusement, before addressing the judge.

'I have no further questions at this stage, my Lord.'

Miller's initial evidence had greatly shocked the crowd; now she had been reduced to a laughing stock within the courtroom. The inference from Scott's highly effective attack had been that she had gone to Perth not to meet Mrs Lockersie, but to bring somebody back to the farm to perhaps teach the farmer a lesson. Her seemingly dishonest description of what had transpired in the byre, and her admission of having slept with the soldier for two nights after being told she was to be rich, had spoken for itself.

Crichton remained the suspect seated within the dock, but the credibility of an apparently lustful and vengeful woman had now been placed firmly alongside him.

In fairly quick succession the prosecution examined several of the witnesses from the vicinity around Mount Stewart Farm to confirm their observations about Crichton. John Sinclair and Jessie McNeil had seen the man ploughing on the day in darkened clothes, but Archibald Harris had seen him 'as white as a doo on the hill'. John Robertson and Robert Dewar in turn deponed that the man was a regular smoker.

The County Constabulary's criminal officers then followed. John Cameron testified how Crichton had told him at the time of the murder that he was not a smoker, only to ask for a smoke several months later on the train following his arrest. George Mearns, having just been promoted to the rank of inspector, described his examination of the cesspool outside the farmhouse, and the lack of any key there at that time.

At half past six in the evening the court now considered James Crichton's evidence, as the declaration he had given to Sheriff Barclay on 17 December was read out to the court. The galleries sat quietly throughout, with all eyes directed to the dock as they listened to the ploughman's account of himself. He would not be questioned further in the court; the declaration would be the one and only chance that he would have to convey to the world his side of the story. With the document read out, the presentation of the prosecution's case was now completed.

It being now close to seven o'clock, the judge ordered the proceedings to be adjourned for the night, to reconvene the next morning at ten o'clock. After the *oath de fideli* was administered to the jurors, they were adjourned and taken to the Salutation Hotel on South Street, where the Young Pretender, Charles Edward Stuart, was said to have stayed over two centuries before, during the Forty-Five campaign, the failed Jacobite rebellion to reclaim the throne for the exiled House of Stuart.

As the jury bedded down for the night, James Crichton was returned once more to the county prison. Commenting on his demeanour, the *Dundee Courier* journalist noted that 'throughout the proceedings of the entire day he listened with greatest attention to all that passed, but never seemed to be excited in the least degree by anything in the evidence bearing more immediately on himself'.

The court reconvened on the morning of Wednesday, 10 April, the *Perthshire Journal and Constitutional* later noting that the chamber was once again crowded with 'an eager and excited audience'. Crichton was once more brought to the bar, with the same paper noting that he 'still preserved the same stolid indifferent air as evinced by him during the whole of Tuesday'.

The exculpatory evidence to be presented by the defence then commenced. To the astonishment of many, the first person to be called was Betsy Riley, whose involvement in the case had been well reported in the early months of the investigation, and who had in recent months become a woman much pilloried in the press as a liar. The hawker was asked to outline her observations on the day of the murder at the farm. As on so many occasions before, the hawker remained adamant that she had seen a gentleman talking to Mrs Rogers by the kitchen door at about half past eleven. Her testimony was brief and not pressed further by Mr Scott, whilst the Advocate Depute's decision not to speak to her at all spoke volumes about the Crown's belief in the credibility of her evidence.

James Crichton's thirteen-year-old son James was then called. He described how his father had worn clean clothes early on the Friday morning, and that in the middle of the day he had returned with a hare that had been caught, though his clothing had remained clean. After his father had washed his hands he had eaten the dinner which had been made ready for him on the table. With the meal completed his mother had then suggested to the ploughman that he should change his clothes, as they were dirty. The lad noted that his father had been wearing a white moleskin jacket and corduroy trousers, but had worn no vest. The jacket had been clean on the night before, following his father's return from the kirk. Having changed his work clothes, Crichton had then remained in the other room, where he had lain down on the floor to have a short nap, not being willing to sleep in the bed during the day. His mother had then commenced her washing later that afternoon, a task which had taken her a couple of hours.

The boy was then asked to recall Christina Miller's stay at his house. He described how, on the Tuesday of that week, both had been out of the house for most of the day. The servant had gone to Dron to see if she could find some work, whilst he had gone to pick up a pre-ordered pair of boots from William Gardiner, the shoemaker at Beautyfield. He noted that he had returned late at night; his mother had already retired to her bed, and both his father and Christina Miller were seated before the fire. He slept with his father that night, he added quickly, for fear that someone might read something else into the situation.

Once the young James had finished giving his evidence, his Dunfermline-based cousin, James Grinton, was brought before the court. When Crichton had been arrested, a small tin tobacco box had been found on his person when searched by John Cameron. The ploughman's nephew stated that he had in fact given his uncle the tobacco box, Crichton having told him that he had some sandpaper and could clean it for him. When the Advocate Depute asked him whether he had bought the box, received it as a present, or found it, Grinton stated that he could not remember, prompting more laughter from the watching public. He added that there was tobacco in the box when he had handed it to his uncle, although he could not remember if the box had been full or empty.

Several more witnesses were interviewed briefly throughout the morning. Thomas Marshall, the shopkeeper at Stanley Provision Store Company, confirmed that he had regularly sold Mrs Rogers snuff, but never tobacco. One of the bags of snuff found at the scene and presented to the court as evidence was readily identified by him as having come from his store. John Smeaton, the soldier who had slept with Christina Miller for two days in Perth, confirmed that he had met the woman whilst in the city. The murder had barely passed in their conversation, other than the fact that he had told her that she would never get the reward, no matter how successful her testimony may prove to be.

Although William Gormack had passed away a few months before, his daughter, Christine, testified to her father's observations of Crichton on the farm on the day of the murder. In particular, she outlined how her father had found it unusual for him to be taking the plough out to the field by the west of the house so late in the afternoon, at almost half past three. The ploughman had previously stated that after his dinner he had removed the posts from the head-ridge of the field, but Henderson had stated this should have taken perhaps half an hour to an hour to achieve. Gormack's evidence had suggested that Crichton had not taken the horses back out until an hour and a half had passed from his break. The inference was that this might have been a window of opportunity within which Crichton may have committed the murder.

To William Henderson's dismay, however, his former neighbour John Ritchie, from Dumbuils Farm, then testified that for Crichton to have removed the posts from the head-ridge of the field where he was working, and to take them back to the farm, could easily have taken an hour and a half to achieve. He would have had to yoke the horse to the cart, lead it to the pile of paling, load the posts, return with them to the yard, empty the cart and then prepare the second horse for the ploughing work. In his mind, the old man's observations of the ploughman were entirely consistent with the task that Crichton had been given.

With the evidence from both the Crown and the defence now presented, it was time for both sides to sum up their perceptions of what had been revealed within the trial. The Advocate Depute, James Adam, addressed the jury on behalf of the prosecution. He described the circumstances by which Janet Rogers' body had been found, before directing the jury that it had one simple question to consider – was James Crichton responsible? There were certain facts that were irrefutable. The murder had occurred between eleven in the forenoon and four o'clock that afternoon, and most likely at around three o'clock, as testified to by Dr Laing. William Henderson could most certainly not have killed his sister, for he had been seen leaving at ten o'clock, and yet a witness had noted Mrs Rogers at the farm's door at midday. It was also clear that Crichton had changed some of his clothes on the Friday on which the murder had happened. He had claimed to have changed his outer items only on that day, having changed his inner garments a week before, and yet the two doctors had both testified that the ploughman's inner clothing had not had a drop of perspiration on them – they too seemed to have been newly put on. Was it also merely a coincidence that Crichton's wife had been washing clothes in the middle of the day?

Adam then turned to the question of whether James Crichton was a smoker or not. Neither Mrs Rogers nor her brother was a smoker – that had been entirely proved – meaning that the pipe and the tin lid found under the bolster at the crime scene had undoubtedly been left by the killer. Crichton had testified that he too had not smoked at that time, but the jury would have to consider whether or not that was the truth. Had Crichton simply claimed this having become aware of the pipe's discovery at the farmhouse? Many witnesses had testified that he had indeed been a smoker. Christina Miller said that the pipe he had used was broken in the shank – as had the shank of the pipe found in the kitchen. The tin lid that the ploughman had on his pipe was also the same as that which Miller had witnessed and indeed used herself before the murder.

Then, the Advocate Depute stated, there was the testimony of Christina Miller herself, on which perhaps the greatest weight should be laid. She had overheard Crichton and his wife state that the ploughman had killed his master's sister. There was no reason why the servant should have accused him of this; she bore no ill will towards him and on the contrary, they had seemed to have been friendly with each other at this time. The reward itself could not have been the motive – she had been arrested to prevent her absconding from the country. He concluded by adding that if the jury believed in the truth of Miss Miller's words, they would have a duty to find the defendant guilty of the charge. He thanked the jury for their time and then took to his seat – little was he aware that he was about to be described by the *Perthshire Journal* as having given 'a very poor speech'.

Charles Scott then rose to summarise the case for the defence. Whilst commending his learned colleague for his sound reasoning over much of the evidence as presented, it was nevertheless his duty to point out the errors within his analysis. Mount Stewart Farm, he suggested, was a house of 'evil omen', a place to which no servant could stay – seven had worked there during the time that Crichton had been employed by William Henderson. Miller had stayed barely a week herself, but it was not for the jury to decide why she had left, or whether she or her master had been telling the full truth over the circumstance. Whatever the reason, a murder had subsequently followed, a brutal killing with unusual ferocity, the victim receiving ten blows to the head with the kitchen axe. This was perhaps not the work of a man in pursuit of plunder at all, he suggested – it could as easily have been the actions of a woman infuriated with passion.

Turning to Crichton, he then suggested that if he was to be considered the killer, did he actually have the opportunity to do so? The answer was undoubtedly yes; however, the jury should not necessarily consider that they had received the full facts. Had anybody else had an opportunity to perform the deed? He suggested that if looking at the word 'opportunity' in its most abstract sense, any person within a three- or four-mile radius of the farm had certainly had an opportunity. It would take only a few minutes to reach the steading, and it was undoubtedly possible for any tramp within the vicinity to have done so. Betsy Riley had seen such a man at the door of the farmhouse, but what of those in the area who may not have been seen? Christina Miller had led a young Irishman called Higgin into the byre with her on the Wednesday night before she had been dismissed. He had spent the night there with the woman, before leaving at five or six o'clock in the morning. Nobody had seen the man come or go, and if he could arrive and leave unseen, it rather proved that so too could another.

The timeline given by James Crichton concerning his movements on the day in question had not been challenged in the slightest. He had ploughed in the field until midday, before returning to Linnlea for his dinner. He had resumed his work at two o'clock, and he had cleared away the posts as required by Henderson. The farmer's neighbour, John Ritchie, had suggested that it could easily take an hour and a half to do so. Crichton had continued to plough until five o'clock after this. By this point the murder had already happened, if the two eminent doctors in attendance shortly after were to be believed. Nobody had countered any of this – and with that as the case the jury could not in all truth claim otherwise in their deliberations either. If the timeline was true, James Crichton was indeed an innocent man.

Scott then turned to the evidence which may be believed to injure such truth. Mrs Crichton had washed clothes on the day of the murder. If there had been no murder, would that have been suspicious? Crichton had changed his clothes in the middle of the day. In the absence of the killing, would that have raised an eyebrow? Two witnesses claimed his clothing to have been dirty in the morning, having seen the ploughman from some 3-400 yards away. Young James Crichton, the labourer's son, had testified that his father had put on clean clothes that morning. He had been in the house beside him. Who would have been better placed to describe the ploughman's clothing on the day in question? Another witness claimed he had looked as 'white as a doo on the hill' whilst out ploughing – but Dr Laing had stated that it did not look as if he had been working at all. Such statements all contradicted each other, and the jury should therefore remember just how subjective the evidence on that front really was.

The final point was Crichton's smoking. The ploughman had stated that at the time he was not a smoker, and yet many had testified to seeing him do so. When the evidence was examined further, it was really apparent that Crichton had meant that he was not a regular smoker. It had been shown from the various shopkeepers in the vicinity that in the space of his six months at Linnlea the ploughman had perhaps purchased no more than two or three ounces of tobacco. The pipe found within the kitchen may indeed have looked similar to the pipe Crichton owned. That did not mean that it was the same implement.

Scott ended his summary with one final and crucial point to which the jury should concern itself. Christina Miller was undoubtedly of bad moral character. How extraordinary was it that the woman could not remember the name of the man she had taken back to the farm and spent the night with in the byre? She had been able to do so for many months, offering the name to the Procurator Fiscal when interviewed, and yet within three weeks of having done so had claimed to have forgotten it once more. That was clearly a lie on which she had called on Almighty God to witness. Should a man be sent to hang on the evidence of a woman not only 'stained with lust', he suggested, but also so clearly a liar? Lying half asleep as she heard Crichton's apparent confession, had she really heard him confess, or had she simply thought that she had? The reward of £100 was also well publicised, and the words she had heard could easily have been twisted as a means to gain such riches.

'Gentlemen,' he said, addressing the jury, 'I put it to you that this is not evidence weighty enough to send the prisoner to the gallows. There is no proof whatsoever that the murder was committed by the accused, and I therefore entreat you to return a verdict of not guilty.'

It was now time for Lord Deas to offer his observations and direction to the jury. It was clear that a murder had occurred, it now remained to be seen whether the prisoner had been the perpetrator. Before considering the case the jury had to be reminded of one pertinent point, the fact that at the outset Crichton had in fact accused William Henderson of the deed. The prisoner had maintained that the farmer had committed the murder after returning to the farm on the evening of Friday, 30 March. The jury must, in their deliberations, establish whether that could have been possible. So many facts, not least of which being the medical evidence, bore against that as a possibility, but it must be considered nonetheless. If Henderson had killed his sister, then clearly his former servant could not have been responsible. If they were satisfied that the farmer was innocent, however, then clearly the ploughman must have known that he was telling a lie. This too should be considered.

Christina Miller's evidence was of paramount importance. There was little doubt that she was not a virtuous woman – but she had never maintained that she was. She had spoken freely about her nights with Higgin and Smeaton. An absence of respectability did not mean an absence of credibility. Their belief in the woman's testimony was crucial, for if they did believe her then her evidence was clearly not just circumstantial but in fact direct testimony that the prisoner had committed the murder.

The jury must also consider the issue surrounding Crichton's clothing and the apparent coincidence of his wife washing in the afternoon. The ploughman's smoking was another issue of equal importance. Miller had claimed that the pipe that had been found at the scene of the crime was similar to that which had been used by Crichton, but she also stated that the broken pipe pieces appeared darker. Were they two separate pipes, or had the pipe found at the scene merely darkened with age over a year and the constant handling by the police and various suspects asked to identify it?

With the summaries now completed, the jurors were directed to retire to a side room to consider their verdict.

—–·—–

Just eleven minutes after their departure, the jurors returned to take their seats within the courtroom, as the watching public and press quietened down once more. The foreman of the jury was asked if they had arrived at a verdict, to which it was confirmed that a decision had been agreed by a majority of twelve to three. He was asked to state the verdict.

'My Lord, the Jury, by a majority, find the Libel not proven.'

The decision was greeted with astonishment by the public. No applause was offered as the ploughman was allowed to leave the dock through the doorway by which he had first been brought in as a prisoner. The Lord Justice Clerk congratulated the sheriffs of both Perthshire and Fifeshire for the splendid way in which they had carried out the administration of justice, and thanked the Lord Provost and local magistrates for their attendance throughout the proceedings. He then commended the city for its magnificent new courthouse, surely the finest in the country. To this comment there was thunderous applause in the chamber. He concluded his speech by thanking the jury for its patience and kind attendance, and stated that the court's business was now concluded. The proceedings were adjourned.

The public left the chamber and, with others gathered on the street outside of the new court building, surrounded the ploughman as he too exited onto the street, where he was joined by his wife and children, as well as several close friends. Members of the press followed in hot pursuit, desperate to gain some kind of reaction from the now freed labourer.

Inside the chamber, William Henderson and his sister's family simply wept.

FIFTEEN

THE SECOND VICTIM

Following the jury's decision, the *Dundee Courier* noted that Perth was to be spared a repetition of the 'dreadful scene which was enacted outside her prison walls on the 22[d] of May last'. The arm of justice had unhappily failed to strike the murderer, it added, though for Crichton 'justice has not, indeed, proclaimed his innocence'. Why had such a verdict been given? Clearly there were 'doubts and bewildering entanglements', it observed, despite the judge's obvious leanings towards a guilty verdict in his summation.

The paper suggested that although it was an unhappy outcome, its salient points were worth examining. Crichton's allegations that William Henderson had killed his sister were clearly nonsense; the farmer's 'very behaviour in court on relating the story of his finding the corpse of his sister must be a strong point in his favour with those who can recognise and rightly estimate the indications of genuine feeling'.

Crichton had displayed himself to be a flawed character; the ploughman had continued to ascertain that he had been a non-smoker at the time of the murder. 'Why this obstinate denial of a fact so well authenticated?' asked the writer. Despite his refutation, the paper conceded that whilst so many facts did circumstantially point towards him as the guilty party, every fact produced could simply have been the mere product of coincidence.

On the other hand, the weight that Lord Deas had given to Christina Miller's testimony was deemed to have been quite extraordinary. Although explored by the defence team, the question of Miller's moral character was a distraction, and avoided something far more fundamental. 'If Crichton really committed the deed, that he should talk thus unreservedly of his crime in the presence of an interested party, without first ascertaining, beyond a doubt, that his words could not reach her, seems to us an act of foolhardiness quite out of keeping with the real character of the man.' Ultimately, the *Courier* suggested, 'either she is a wilful liar, or he is a wilful murderer'.

In a separate column within the same edition, the paper did add one further outcome from the trial. A single newsagent in Dundee had sold 1,300 editions of the *Dundee Courier and Argus*, and could have sold several hundred more if he had been able to receive additional copies. The title stated that it had indeed printed a much higher run of the paper, but that the sales had far exceeded its calculations. Whilst justice may or may not have been served, the court proceedings had certainly been good for business.

Closer to the seat of the trial, the *Perthshire Courier* believed that the verdict was acceptable, though was surprised that the case 'did not result in a more exonerating finding'. Of the prior investigation it was much more critical. 'If after even half a year's delay and upwards such a case could be made up as was laid before the court last week; what kind of a case, we ask, might not reasonably be expected to have been prepared had the matter been shrewdly gone about at the moment?'

The paper noted that hindsight was a wonderful thing, but that the County Constabulary clearly had lessons to learn. 'What reason was there for so much tardiness and tenderness, and for so large a display of that charity which thinketh no evil, we do not know; but it would materially relieve this question of much of the painful perplexity in which it is involved if some good reason could be adduced for not doing at the time what was done with almost success afterwards.' It concluded its diatribe by adding, 'it is a circumstance calling for something more than grudge that a respectable woman should be brutally slaughtered in her brother's house, in broad daylight, in a comparatively thickly populated and open district of country, and that all that can be got is a verdict of not proven.'

After an immediate report on the trial published on Thursday, 11 April, the *Perthshire Advertiser* considered the verdict in much further detail a week later. It was under no doubt that the circumstances of the case had pointed very firmly towards Crichton as having been guilty. But, the paper asked, 'which of our readers has not been at fault in his interpretation of circumstances? Is there one who can honestly say he has not been mislaid by them?' It observed that the verdict had 'collided with the natural instinct of retaliation or revenge', noting that such an instinct had formed the basis of law for many from before the time of Moses. Retaliation, however, was not the same thing as justice.

The killer, whoever he was, had undoubtedly walked free, despite having been 'searched for as with lighted candles', though the paper added that it was likely that he had 'got a fright he will never forget'. It even suggested, with extraordinary optimism, that it would be unlikely that he would repeat his crimes, and that the weight of the deed on the killer's own conscience might perhaps be justice enough. Hanging would have been instant, but living with the actions he had performed on that day would haunt the murderer for the rest of his life.

This analysis provoked some outrage in Perth. In a follow-up letter published on 2 May, one of the paper's readers, writing as 'Pro Bono Publico', agreed with some of the journalist's assertions, but added that the paper's readers would be easily aware that 'for days – for weeks – even for months, the efforts put forth to secure the murderer or murderers, seemed, in the eyes of the public, little else than a display of the merest official imbecility'. He did not doubt that the investigation had been 'as with lighted candles' but suggested that 'in a search where matters of life and death are involved, its effectiveness depends as much upon the time when the candles are lighted as upon the brilliance with which they burn after being lighted.'

The writer was firmly of the opinion that the police methodology employed had been thoroughly incompetent: 'when it became known that Mrs Rodgers [*sic*] had been murdered it seemed as if, in such a case, the watching of the lifeless body was the only thing which came within the province of our detective force.'

The concluding paragraph was equally devastating: 'It is clear that our relatives may be murdered at our own firesides at noon-day. Our door-neighbours may immediately thereafter denude themselves of their clothing, to the last shred, and sally forth into the fields in an unusual garb, and at an unusual hour. The inhabitants of the surrounding neighbourhood may feel astonished; while, under the very nose of our constabulary, the wives may soak, wash and bleach the filthy garments their husbands have just doffed; but, nevertheless, their dwellings must be held too sacred to be defiled by the tread of a policeman's foot!' The writer concluded that in all of his experiences in criminal cases, he had yet to come across one so 'bungled'; he hoped never to again.

——•——

For Chief Constable Gordon and the County Constabulary such criticism made for uncomfortable reading. Although the investigation remained open, the Mount Stewart murderer was never to be caught. There were no further arrests; no additional clues were discovered; and no more interest in it was shown by the press. The suspicion surrounding James Crichton remained that, and no more.

Some called for the ploughman to be retried, but in its article on Thursday, 18 April, the *Perthshire Advertiser* pointed out that, 'A person once tried . . . cannot be tried again for the same crime, whether the verdict which dismissed him was Not Guilty or Not Proven'. The paper did suggest one possibility – the idea that although he could not be tried for murder, if sufficient evidence was discovered, there was nothing to stop the labourer being charged for burglary or some other related offence. No such evidence was ever found; the world moved on.

In the immediate aftermath of the trial, Crichton was certainly a persecuted man. The *Dundee Courier and Argus* noted on Saturday, 13 April, that on the previous day a respectable-looking man had been passing Dudhope Free Church on the way to Lochee. A crowd had run up to him, with one shouting, 'That's Crichton, the murderer!' The paper had not been able to establish if it had actually been the ploughman, though reported that the gentleman himself had certainly not denied it. The crowd was thus further angered and began to hiss and shout at him until he was forced to seek shelter in a grocer's shop. There he remained until the rabble had dispersed. The paper also reported that another gentleman showing a likeness to Crichton had been tormented by a mob on the Perth Road later that evening, though he had later turned out to be a residenter on Miller's Wynd.

How injured James Crichton was by the stigma of association with the murder, we will never know. He survived for another twenty-seven years, continuing to work as an agricultural labourer and then in his latter years as a road surfaceman in his native Fife. He passed away at Milton, in the village of Markinch, on 6 April 1894.

What became of Christina Miller has never been established. She most certainly did not receive a reward for her contribution to the investigation, and whether she did set sail for America is equally unknown. The suggestion in the court that the attack on Janet Rogers was just as likely to have been caused by a woman 'infuriated with passion' had clearly been a suggestion that there might have been more to Miller's involvement than previously considered; but the theory was never tested.

The hawker, Betsy Riley, continued to reside in Perth with her ill husband. Had she misled the force for months, or had she stared into the very face of the killer shortly before the death of Janet Rogers? Whether she had been honest with the court or not was never resolved; she took the truth with her to the grave on 1 June 1872, aged just fifty-five years.

For Chief Constable Gordon, the case would remain the only unsolved murder during his long tenure with the force. He continued in his post for another ten years, until his sudden death on 23 June 1877. Despite the failure of the investigation he had utterly transformed his police force, for which he has been so rightly commemorated by those who succeeded him. The Perthshire Constabulary had been professionalised and better accommodation and terms had been secured for those who had served under him. He had set up an embryonic criminal investigation department within his force just two years before the murder, and had thrown all the resources that he had possessed into trying to locate the killer. With an unhappy result at the outcome of the trial, the finger of blame had been quickly pointed at both he and his force; but this was the age before forensic science, fingerprints and DNA evidence. It was quite possibly a case that could simply not be resolved, no matter which techniques may have been applied at the time. It technically remains an open investigation to this day with the constabulary's successor, Tayside Police Force; but it will never be solved.

Janet Rogers was the tragic victim of the Mount Stewart Murder of 1866, a tale followed for just over a year by interested readers from the shipyards of Belfast to the fishing boats of Aberdeen, and from the slums of Dublin to the capital of the British Empire at London. As so often happens, however, tragedy can beget further tragedy, and this story would not end quite so abruptly. Janet Rogers was the tragic victim of the Mount Stewart Murder – but she was not the only victim.

The anonymous killer had one more soul yet to claim.

Three weeks after the trial, on 2 May 1867, a reader of the *Perthshire Advertiser* wished to comment on the treatment of Janet Rogers' brother, William Henderson. Identified only as 'B.I.', the writer observed that the farmer had suffered 'a gross injury in purse, person and character', and how he as a spectator had 'found himself often scandalised by the heartlessness with which this gentleman was treated'. Not only had Henderson been made to endure the ordeal of finding his dead sister, but suspicion had then been cast upon him as the possible culprit for her death. 'Life cannot be brought back to the clay,' noted the writer, 'yet reparation may be made to the living; and I think that in the spirit of true religion, a debt is due here, where offence has been so heavy.'

The writer was not merely commenting on Henderson's treatment throughout the investigation and trial. On the day following Crichton's acquittal, the farmer had once more travelled from Perth to Mount Stewart Farm, so that he might speak to several of the witnesses and look around his former property one last time. His motivation for doing so lay with the evidence given by one of the witnesses at the trial. John Ritchie of Dumbuils had maintained that it would have taken Crichton an hour and a half to clear the head-ridge of the posts on the field where the ploughman had been working on the day of the killing. Henderson had been furious at the suggestion, and at the Bridge of Earn had told Constable Cumming that he believed Ritchie had perjured himself during the trial. He repeated the same allegation to James Williamson at Carmichael Cottages, and to Peter Stewart, now the farmer at Mount Stewart. On his return to Perth the farmer had also made the same claim to John Peters, the clerk in the Sheriff Clerk's Office.

On Tuesday, 23 April 1867, John Ritchie sued Henderson for slander at the Perth Small Debt Court. Henry Whyte, the solicitor who had advised the defence team for Crichton during the trial, acted for Ritchie in the pursuit of £12 sterling of damages. The case was heard before Sheriff Barclay, who threw out the first charge relating to the discussion made with the constable. On the remaining allegations – that Henderson had made the claim in discussion with Peter Stewart and James Williamson – the farmer was found guilty. He was ordered to pay thirty shillings in damages, the slander having been found to be false, malicious, injurious and calumnious. Barclay had not been an unfeeling man; he had reduced the damages in mitigation of the fact that it had been Henderson's sister who had been murdered. Any display of feeling on his part was most certainly not justifiable, the sheriff decreed, but under the circumstances the farmer was perhaps entitled to some excuse for his lapse in judgement.

There is no record of what Henderson experienced in the immediate aftermath of the two court cases. Whatever sufferings he endured as a result of Crichton's acquittal were known only to him and perhaps a few close members of his family. He certainly continued to meet regularly in Perth with his uncle, Dr William Henderson, to whom he was a favoured nephew. The physician, a wealthy man who, like the former procurator fiscal John McLean, had lived for many years on the city's Rose Terrace, had no children of his own. Following the death of his wife he had been cared for by his niece, Eliza Henderson, until she had married Archibald McDonald, purportedly the illegitimate son of Sir John McDonald of Dalchosnie, in 1868. The two single Henderson men, sharing both a forename and the same blood, spoke regularly on many matters, and were glad for the other's company.

In May 1870, Dr Henderson decided to record his will. At eighty-six years old, he was well aware that time was becoming more precious by the day, and so had wished to set up a trust from which his estate could be administered in the aftermath of his death. To run this trust he turned to a close friend, George Gray, a notary in the city, and to the three closest members of his family – the Reverend Andrew Henderson Anderson, son of his sister Isobel; Eliza's husband, Archibald McDonald; and William Henderson.

The doctor desired for the four gentlemen to carry out two key functions following his death. Six months after he had passed away he wished for them to make certain legacy gifts available from his estate to his family members and closest friends. Amongst such gifts, his nephew William Henderson was to receive £1,000, whilst Janet Rogers' daughter, Ann, was to receive all of his apparel and £100. The rest of Janet's daughters were to each receive £50.

Secondly, the physician asked his trustees to manage a fund that he wished to set up for the administration of the poor of Perthshire. 'Dr William Henderson's Mortification' was to be established with a legacy of £6,000, and would primarily benefit those from his home parish of Kinclaven, who shared the surname of Henderson, or who were in some way able to prove that they were related to him.

Within the next month, however, something happened between the doctor and his favoured nephew. Whatever the disagreement or change of circumstance had been, the physician issued a codicil, or correction to the will, dramatically reducing his nephew's involvement in the management of his estate. The legacy of £1,000 was to be cut to just £600; furthermore, the former farmer was no longer to be a trustee of the mortification fund. No reason was ever given, or has ever been discovered, and the physician died just a few months later, on 13 October 1870.

The good doctor had clearly reconsidered the suitability of his nephew to take on the responsibility initially asked of him. As a physician he had been much respected in the city, with his medical skills internationally recognised. While we cannot know why he had made such a dramatic change to his will, it is entirely possible that his medical judgements had caught a glimpse of a new tragedy that was about to unfold.

By the time of his uncle's death, Henderson had already relocated to New Scone on the east side of the Tay from Perth, living the life of a feuar. He was financially secured, and settled at a substantial eight-roomed property amidst heavily planted orchards at Belford Place, on the village's Lynedoch Road. In addition to his own house, he also held an adjacent property on the Murrayhall estate, comprised of a house, garden, gig and workshop, which he rented out annually. His tenants over the next decade would include a corn merchant, a dentist, a potato merchant and a commission agent.

Despite the quiet, rural beauty of his surroundings, all was not well with William Henderson. In the opening days of May 1881, the retired farmer's neighbours had started to notice that he was not of a correct frame of mind, with one visitor to his property sufficiently alarmed enough to inform the local constable, who lived just a couple of cottages away. Finding that there was cause for concern, the Murray Royal Lunatic Asylum was duly alerted, the local hospital for the care of the insane which had been built in 1825 by James Murray, a resident from Perth who had inherited a vast fortune following the death of a relation in India. On Tuesday, 17 May, a Dr Augustus Barclay Calder from the institution visited Henderson at his home in Belford Place, and in a detailed report noted that his disposition was melancholic and reserved. Although described by many as steady, industrious and temperate, the doctor found him to be 'cleanly, but untidy'.

Henderson's mind was in a fragile state. He was 'at present in a state of Mental Derangement', having been insane for about ten days. 'He talks constantly and incoherently,' noted the physician, adding that he 'cries for the police without due reason.' More disturbingly, the retired farmer was talking nonsense about harm that had allegedly been carried out against his body: 'Says his entrails have been removed, and buried in McLeish's Place'.

William's sister Isobel, with her husband Peter, was called to assist and remained with her brother for a couple of days to try to soothe his troubled mind. On Thursday, 19 May, a second opinion was given by another physician, Howard Bendall, who again visited Henderson at home. He too found the farmer to be mentally unsound. 'He rambles from subject to subject in conversation, and is inconsequent in his answers to questions,' observed Bendall. 'He states that he has been poisoned this morning by the attendant in charge, and requested me to use the stomach pump for removal of the poison'.

On 20 May 1881, Melville Jameson, John McLean's successor as procurator fiscal, petitioned Sheriff Substitute Hugh Barclay to have Henderson placed into the asylum. Barclay had been shocked to learn of Henderson's condition, recalling the terrible ordeal that had befallen the man some fifteen years earlier. An ex-officio director of the institution himself from as far back as 1834, Barclay readily agreed to the detention, for which the Health Board would be charged £50 per quarter.

The farmer was held at the asylum for three months. The medical report within the hospital's Register of Physical Condition painted a tragic picture of the recent lifestyle endured by the once proud farmer, noting that he had always been 'peculiar' and 'of late years more so'. He lived 'alone in a miserly way', was 'melancholic and reserved in disposition', although 'steady and industrious'. This was his first ever mental breakdown, and the register recorded its cause: 'About ten days ago became excited in consequence of a dispute about a cess-pool. This excitement was much increased and he became raving and frantic. Cries for police and protection.'

The state of his mind was described as 'excited and incoherent', with Henderson constantly screaming that he wished for protection from the police. 'Want old reports, send for the key'. Refers continually to the murder of his sister for which he was apprehended and acquitted 15 years ago. In a state of acute mania.'

As well as his mental deterioration, Henderson was also by now a physically ill man. His bowels were not working properly, and he was forced to have an enema. He had a cough and was constantly producing bronchitic spit. Within a week at the institution his body began to recover, but not his mind. The questioning about the murder continued, as he talked constantly of the evidence that had been presented at the trial, and the finding of the key in the cesspool.

On 10 June 1881, Henderson was observed to be under the delusion that he was being kept against his will. Eleven days later he stated that there was nothing the matter with him, and that all of the excitement that had led him to the asylum had been caused by the local constable setting everybody against him. On 23 June the doctor noted that he continued to be 'diffusive and loquacious' as the New Scone resident vowed 'vengeance against the Inspector of the Poor and the Policeman for causing all his excitement and incarceration'. He complained that his garden would be so ruined that nobody would be able to get into it, and he screamed that the key was being hidden. He believed that his friends had placed him in the asylum as a means to secure his money.

On 16 August 1881, Henderson was believed to have recovered sufficiently enough to be discharged to the care of his nephew in Blackford, William Hay Paton, husband of his niece Janet Rogers. With his nieces Janet and Ann to help care for him, it was hoped that his sufferings would be eased. For a time they perhaps were, but the medical reports show that the tranquillity within his mind would not last.

In October 1882, Henderson was recorded as having been met on the street by a reporter, 'full of delusions as to people annoying him, threatening law proceedings, and making irrational references to his sister's murder'. He was returned to his house in New Scone, out of sight and out of his mind.

On 26 August 1884, Henderson was re-admitted to the asylum, having been arrested by the police, who had found the deranged man smashing windows in Crieff. At the local prison in Perth he was examined by two physicians, Dr David Fleming and Dr Robert Christie. They noted that following his previous discharge from the asylum he had suffered a hemiplegic seizure, most likely caused by a stroke, which had paralysed a great part of the right side of his body.

Fleming described his recent condition in a medical certificate issued on the day. 'I have known him for long, and visited often, during the whole time he has been weak minded and jealous of those around him. Today he talks incessantly but on no subject in particular. All he says is downright nonsense.' Christie concurred. 'He talks in an incoherent and rambling manner, seems quite unconscious of anything said to him.' There were several categories of mental derangement. Henderson was not a 'lunatic', or an 'insane person', nor was he an 'idiot' – instead, he was judged to be 'of unsound mind'.

On the same day that he was examined, his brother-in-law, Peter Anderson, petitioned to have him committed back into the asylum. In the application, Anderson noted that he had resided at several places after his previous discharge from the institution. With the request granted by the sheriff, Henderson was re-admitted.

By now his physical condition had deteriorated much further. The old man was suffering from cardiac exhaustion, the doctors noting that his heartbeat was 'scarcely audible'. His legs were heavily ulcerated; his right arm and the left side of his face bruised; his teeth virtually all gone, along with his appetite. His motion and sensation were severely impaired, and he was infested with lice. Tellingly, his initial examination by the medical staff had to be postponed due to his 'maniacal state'.

For the first two weeks inside his ward, William remained confined to a bed with side railings attached to prevent him falling out and hurting himself. He was noted as 'wet, dirty, destructive, raving, restless', with his condition not quietening until the second week of September. At this point he experienced a sudden improvement, though any excitement 'makes his speech more imperfect from paralysis'. It was not to last. By 15 December he was once again in a bad way, talking non-stop 'about the Bible, intermixed with rough language'.

For six long years, William Henderson's state varied from month to month. At several stages he was confined to his bed, at others he was able to sit up in a chair. A record from 7 April 1886 states 'his temper is very variable, sometimes he is very good natured, and laughs childishly a little, at others he is very noisy and swears a great deal', with the physician noting three months later that he had improved so much he no longer disturbed others sleeping in the dormitory at night. The once proud farmer was nevertheless a broken man. He was 'weakminded' and 'occasionally wets himself during the day and occasionally is dirty at night'.

By the end of May the farmer was again totally incoherent and spent every day simply seated in his chair. He was 'very troublesome to dress at times' and on 27 December 1887 noted as having been confined to bed for the previous month, 'as a swelling appeared over his right pectoral muscle evidently from pulling about when being dressed'.

Henderson's mental faculties continued to retreat further from the real world. In his own mind he continued to fight hard for the justice that had evaded the sister he had loved so dearly. The key in the cesspool had clearly been planted by the killer; but nobody was listening. James Crichton had killed Janet, and was laughing in the face of those who had sought to see him brought to justice; but nobody was listening. The establishment was incompetent, it was inherently evil; but nobody was listening. In time his mental state deteriorated so far that not even he could listen. The farmer plummeted towards his own personal oblivion.

On 5 March 1888, Henderson experienced a series of fits on four occasions between 1 a.m. and 2 a.m. He was unconscious throughout, but each fit commenced with a slight cry, before leading him to foam at the mouth and pass water as his body convulsed. It was bizarrely noted that as a result of his seizures his speech ability actually improved. On 12 June he had another similar attack, and whatever mental ability he still had appears to have finally deserted him. A note on 10 October recorded that he could 'only say "Old Devil"' and 'lies grinning and moving his hand'.

Throughout 1889, Henderson remained bedridden and 'happy as a rule'. Towards the end of the year his body finally began to give way. He developed bedsores on his back which were initially healed with creolin ointment, but his legs were 'much drawn up and extension by a weight and pulley applied', with little effect. The sores returned and worsened, refusing to heal, no matter which poultices were offered. His appetite soon disappeared completely.

At half past nine in the morning on 22 January 1890, Henderson suddenly collapsed in his bed, very pale and with a feeble pulse. Alcohol was applied to try to stimulate him, but his body finally failed. At 11.25 a.m., aged seventy-seven, William Henderson passed away. An attendant in the asylum informed the registrar about his death. There was no coverage in the newspaper, no fancy funeral.

The Mount Stewart murderer had claimed his second victim.

AFTERWORD

Despite the tragedy of Janet Rogers' murder, the family story continued.

Janet's widower, James Rogers, continued to live in his home village of Airntully until his death following a heart attack on Saturday, 13 March 1875. Together, James and his wife had brought five daughters into the world, successfully raising them as a loving family within their Perthshire home, and through them the couple's story continued to thrive.

Their eldest child, also called Janet, had married a currier by the name of William Hay Paton at the United Presbyterian manse of Kinclaven in 1859. After a brief five-year spell residing within the thriving metropolis of Glasgow the couple had returned to their native Perthshire, settling in the quiet town of Blackford, where they would spend the next twenty years feeding, clothing and inspiring their own family of nine children. Only three of their children were alive when Janet was murdered in 1866, the eldest boy, James, being just six years old. In the years to come the children were told endless stories of their fun-loving grandmother, rather than of the tragic victim that she became at the hands of a heartless killer.

Ann Rogers, who had resided with her parents at Airntully in 1866, stayed with her father until his death in 1875. Her eyesight continued to deteriorate, and after James' eventual passing she moved to Blackford to live a couple of doors away from her sister Janet. Ann never married, and when the Patons moved back to Glasgow in the 1880s, she accompanied them, eventually passing away in their tenement flat on the city's Springfield Road in October 1895. Janet survived herself for another eleven years until nature took its eventual course in November 1906.

The children of Janet and William went on to achieve many great things; some remained in Scotland, whilst others ventured further afield. Their eldest son, James Paton, moved to London to work as a manager for the Singer Sewing Machine Company. His own son, William, would in time end up as secretary of the International Missionary Society, counting Mahatma Ghandi amongst the many dignitaries with whom he would often share conversation, whilst his grandson, Sir William Paton, would teach pharmacology at Oxford University. Another grandson, David, would serve for eleven years as a chaplain to Queen Elizabeth II and as a canon in Canterbury Cathedral.

The third son of Janet and William, David Hepburn Paton, married Inverness lass Jessie MacFarlane in 1888. With her he raised a family of four in Brussels, Belgium, where for almost thirty years he managed several shoe shops on behalf of a Glaswegian firm called R. and J. Dicks. This grandson of Janet Rogers would suffer immense tragedy in his own right. During the German occupation of the city in the First World War, he went into hiding for sixteen months to avoid being interned as an enemy civilian. By 1916 the war had taken its toll – the stress of his situation became too much and David collapsed and died in the safe house where he was staying. His body was subsequently thrown out onto the street in order that those who had hidden him would not be seen to be collaborators; his final resting spot has never been located. Following David's death, his brother James acted as a vital lifeline from London for his widow Jessie and her children, who remained trapped in Brussels throughout the rest of the war, before their eventual return to Scotland following the Armistice.

David's youngest son, Charles Paton, survived the hardships of the occupation and moved to Northern Ireland in 1936, after marrying a Glaswegian woman, Jean Currie, with whom he would have three sons and a daughter. Charles survived the Belfast Blitz of 1941, when his house in the city's Whitewell district was damaged by a German bomb, and he later served as a member of the Royal Air Force Volunteer Reserve. His marriage would not survive, with the couple separating in the 1950s. Charles eventually passed away in the small Ulster town of Donaghadee in September 1987.

The youngest son of Charles and Jean, Colin Paton, grew up in Carrickfergus, County Antrim, before leaving the quiet seaside town to travel the world with the Royal Navy. With the luck of the Irish, he narrowly avoided death during the Cold War, when his submarine was involved in a collision with a Russian counterpart in the Barents Sea. Some thirty years later, as a guard on a First Great Western train bound for London in 1999, he was again fortunate to survive the deadly crash at Ladbroke Grove. Of his five children, the eldest son – and author of this work – would return to live in Scotland with his own wife, Claire Giles, and in turn have two sons, Calum and Jamie. They continue to live there to this day.

The tragedy of Janet Rogers' untimely demise deprived her of the dignity of old age, but it did not deprive her of her greatest achievement, the family that survived her. It is hoped that this work can somehow pay tribute to the strength of those who lived through the ordeal of 1866, to continue the story of that family which carries on to this very day.

May Janet, and her brother William, rest in peace.

BIBLIOGRAPHY

Newspapers

Mount Stewart Murder

Aberdeen Herald: 1866 – 7 Apr, 14 Apr, 21 Apr, 28 Apr, 26 May

Aberdeen Journal: 1866 – 4 Apr, 18 Apr, 25 Apr, 2 May; 1867 – 1 May

Belfast Newsletter: 1866 – 23 Apr

Caledonian Mercury: 1866 – 3 Apr, 11 May, 18 Dec, 22 Dec; 1867 – 10 Apr, 11 Apr, 12 Apr, 13 Apr

Cheshire Observer: 1866 – 7 Apr

Daily News: 1866 – 3 Apr

Dundee Advertiser: 1866 – 3 Apr

Dundee Courier and Argus: 1866 – 2 Apr, 5 Apr, 12 Apr, 21 Apr, 23 Apr, 18 Dec, 19 Dec, 22 Dec, 24 Dec; 1867 – 10 Jan, 9 Apr, 10 Apr, 11 Apr, 13 Apr, 24 Apr

Glasgow Daily Herald: 1866 – 2 Apr, 3 Apr, 12 Apr, 21 Apr, 18 Dec, 25 Dec; 1867 – 10 Apr

Illustrated Police News: 1867 – 13 Apr

Lancaster Gazette: 1866 – 7 Apr

Leeds Mercury: 1866 – 3 Apr, 18 Dec; 1867 – 11 Jan

Liverpool Mercury: 1867 – 12 Apr

London Standard: 1866 – 3 Apr

Morning Post: 1866 – 4 Apr

North British Daily Mail: 1866 – 2 Apr, 5 Apr

Perthshire Advertiser: 1866 – 5 Apr, 12 Apr, 19 Apr, 26 Apr; 1867 – 11 Apr, 18 Apr, 2 May; 2006 – 17 Nov

Perthshire Courier: 1866 – 3 Apr, 17 Apr, 24 Apr, 22 May, 29 May; 1867 – 16 Apr, 30 Apr, 26 May

Perthshire Journal and Constitutional: 1866 – 5 Apr, 11 Apr, 12 Apr, 19 Apr, 26 Apr, 20 Dec, 27 Dec; 1867 – 10 Jan, 11 Apr, 12 Apr, 25 Apr

Police Gazette: 1866 – 9 Apr, 16 Apr

Preston Guardian: 1866 – 21 Apr
The Scotsman: 1866 – 2 Apr, 3 Apr, 4 Apr, 5 Apr, 12 Apr, 19 Apr, 23 Apr; 1867 – 10 Apr
Sheffield and Rotherham Independent: 1866 – 3 Apr
The Times: 1867 – Apr 11
York Herald: 1866 – 7 Apr

Blairingone murder
Belfast Newsletter: 1866 – 24 May
Caledonian Mercury: 1866 – 2 Apr
Dundee Courier: 1866 – 10 Apr, 18 Apr, 24 Apr, 25 Apr, 26 Apr, 23 May,
Glasgow Herald: 1866 – 26 Apr, 22 May
Perthshire Journal and Constitutional: 1866 – 24 May, 26 May

Scott murder
Aberdeen Journal: 1866 – 11 Apr
Caledonian Mercury: 1866 – 10 Apr, 19 Apr
Glasgow Herald: 1866 – 12 Apr

Janet Anderson murder
Perthshire Advertiser: 1849 – 3 May, 10 May, 31 May

Cattle plague
Caledonian Mercury: 1865 – 23 Sep, 31 Oct
Dundee Courier and Argus: 1865 – 1 Nov
Perth Courier: 1866 – 10 Apr
Pall Mall Gazette: 1865 – 1 Aug

Murray Royal Lunatic Asylum
Caledonian Mercury: 1830 – 30 Apr

Books

Barclay, Hugh. *A Digest of the Law of Scotland, with Special Reference to the Offices and Duties of a Justice of the Peace (2nd edition)*. 1855

Bell, William. *A Dictionary and Digest of the Law of Scotland*. 1838

Blair, William. *The Scottish Justices Manual; being an Alphabetical Compendium of the Powers and Duties of the Justices of the Peace within Scotland*. 1834

Clark, Robert. *A View of the Office of Sheriff*. 1824

Cumming, Revd Alexander. Parish of Dunbarny (2nd Statistcial Account). 1842

Drummond, Revd James. Parish of Forgandenny (2nd Statistical Account). 1843

Findlay, W.H. *Heritage of Perth*. 1984

Gibb, A.D. *Students' Glossary of Scottish Legal Terms*. 1946

Lindsay, W.L. *General History of the Murray Royal Institution (for the Insane) Perth*. 1878

MacFarlane, Willie. *The History of the Perthshire and Kinross-Shire Constabularies*. 2011

Marshal, James. *The Post Office Perth Directory 1866-67 and Other Useful Information*. 1866

May, Trevor. *The Victorian Undertaker*. 1996

Omand, Donald. *The Perthshire Book*. 1999

Penny, George. *Traditions of Perth*. 1836

Pupils of Primary VI of Caledonian Road School. *What's in a Name: A Survey of Perth Street Names*. 1979

Ross, Gregory. *Forgandenny: A Place in History.* 2007

Seath, J.W. & R.E. *Dunbarney: A Parish with a Past.* 1991

Tod, T.M. *The Scots Black Kalendar.* 1938

Wilson, Sir James. *Lowland Scotch as Spoken in the Lower Strathearn District of Perthshire.* 1915

Documentary resources

National Records of Scotland

Mount Stewart Murder trial papers:

Precognition papers	AD14/67/170
Minutes: JC11/104 p.26r	
Case papers	JC26/1867/20
Architect plans	RHP141081/1-2

Perth and Kinross Archives

Perthshire Constabulary papers:

POL 1/2/2	General Order Book
POL 1/5/3	Letter book 1862-67
POL 1/16/1	1845-80 Constables
POL 1/18/1	Register of Officers and Constables
POL 1/36/2	Arrest book
POL 1/38/3	Charge book

University of Dundee Archive Services

Murray Royal Hospital papers:

THB 29/8/2/10	Petitions for Admission Vol. 11 1880–84
THB 29/8/6/2	Patient case books and case files
THB 29/8/12/1	Address Books

ABOUT THE AUTHOR

Chris Paton is a former BBC Scotland television producer/director specialising in history-based programmes. He holds a Postgraduate Diploma in Genealogical Studies and runs the Scotland's Greatest Story family history service. He has regularly written for *Ancestors*, *Discover my Past Scotland*, *Family History Monthly*, *Family Tree*, *History Scotland*, *Irish Roots*, *Practical Family History*, *Your Family History*, *Your Family Tree*, and his own British GENES (Genealogy News and Events) blog at http://britishgenes.blogspot.com. He lives in North Ayrshire, in the west of Scotland.

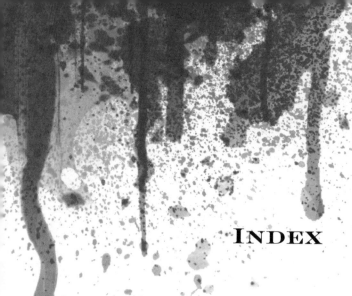

INDEX